EASY PIANO

CHRISTIAN POP/ROCK

MW00682300

2   DIVE | **STEVEN CURTIS CHAPMAN**

14   EVERLASTING GOD | **LINCOLN BREWSTER**

9   GET DOWN | **AUDIO ADRENALINE**

18   HOLY | **NICHOLE NORDEMAN**

23   LEARNING TO BREATHE | **SWITCHFOOT**

30   LET IT FADE | **JEREMY CAMP**

42   MADE TO LOVE | **TOBYMAC**

48   ONLY GRACE | **MATTHEW WEST**

37   REVELATION | **THIRD DAY**

54   SEA OF FACES | **KUTLESS**

60   SHINE | **NEWSBOYS**

66   SONG OF LOVE | **REBECCA ST. JAMES**

75   TAKE YOU AT YOUR WORD | **AVALON**

70   YOU ARE THE ANSWER | **POINT OF GRACE**

ISBN 978-0-4234-8770-8

HAL•LEONARD®
CORPORATION
7777 W. BLUEMOUND RD. P.O. BOX 13819 MILWAUKEE, WI 53213

Visit Hal Leonard Online at
www.halleonard.com

DIVE

Words and Music by
STEVEN CURTIS CHAPMAN

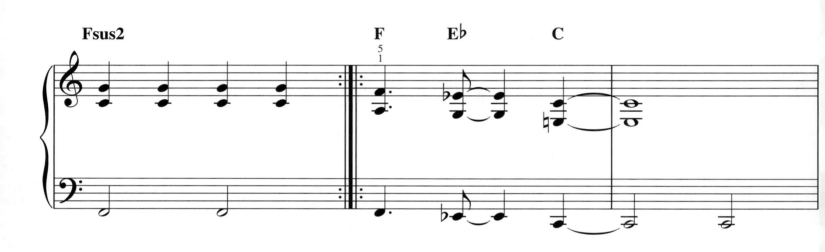

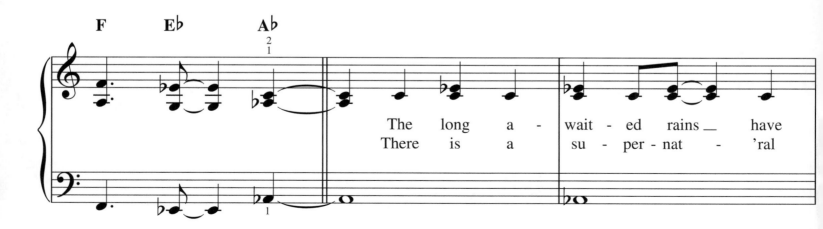

The long a - wait - ed rains __ have
There is a su - per - nat - 'ral

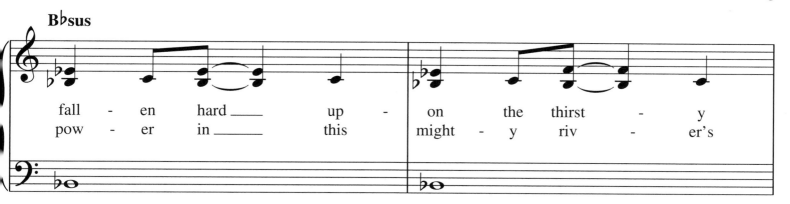

B♭sus

fall - en hard ____ up - on the thirst - y
pow - er in ____ this might - y riv - er's

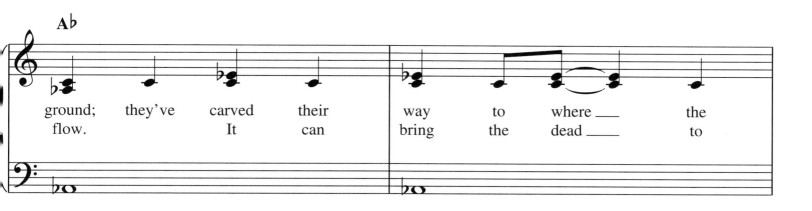

A♭

ground; they've carved their way to where ____ the
flow. It can bring the dead ____ to

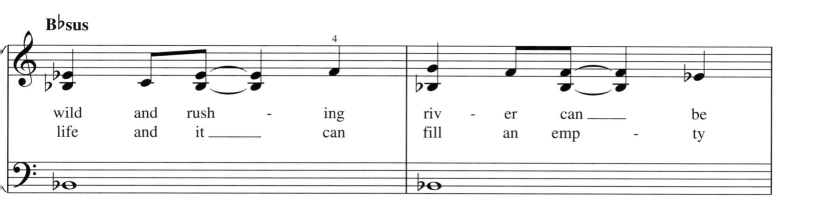

B♭sus

wild and rush - ing riv - er can ____ be
life and it ____ can fill an emp - ty

A♭

found. And like the rain, I have ____ been
soul, and give our hearts the on - ly

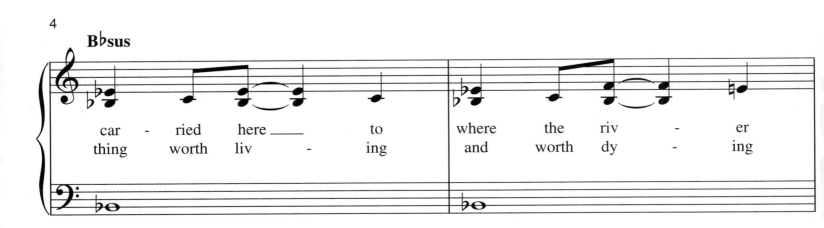

B♭sus

car - ried here ____ to where the riv - er
thing worth liv - ing and worth dy - ing

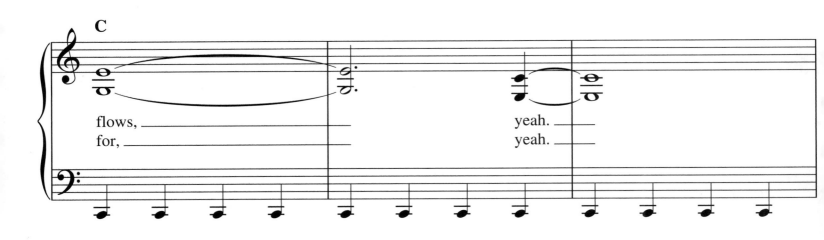

C

flows, ____ ____ yeah. ____
for, ____ ____ yeah. ____

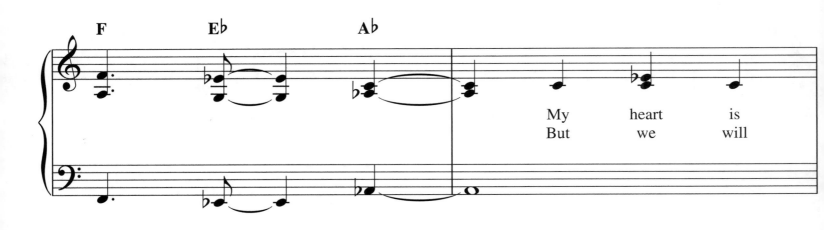

F   **E♭**   **A♭**

My heart is
But we will

B♭sus

rac - ing and ____ my knees are weak ____ as
nev - er know ____ the awe - some pow - er

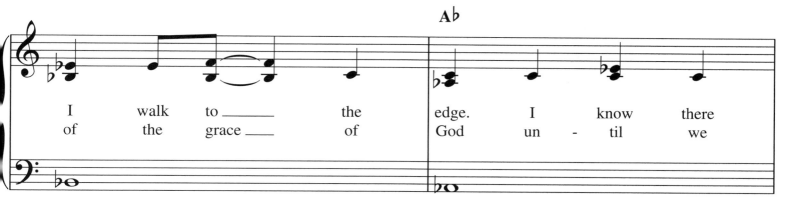

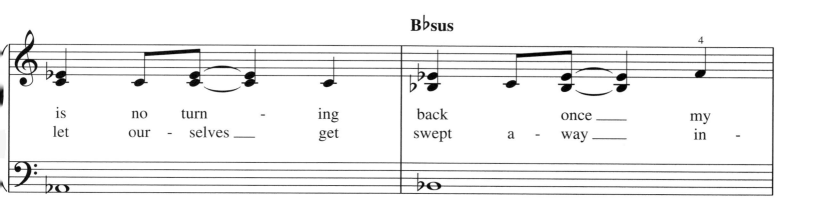

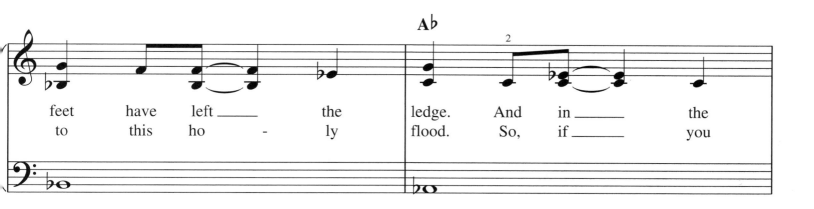

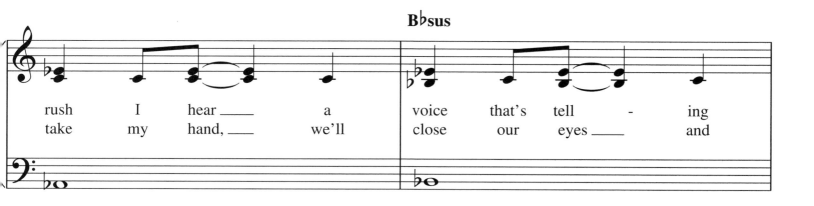

6

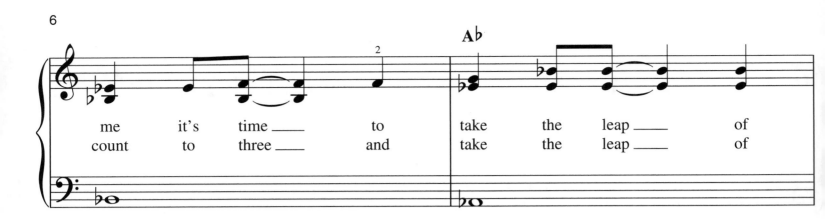

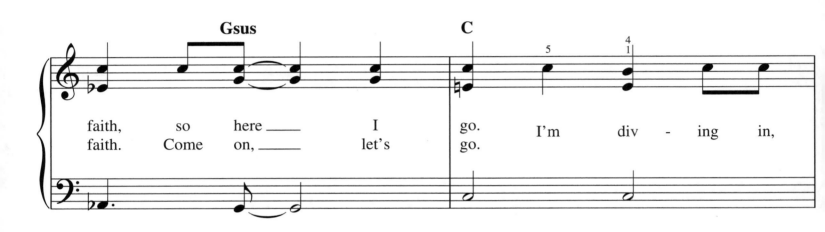

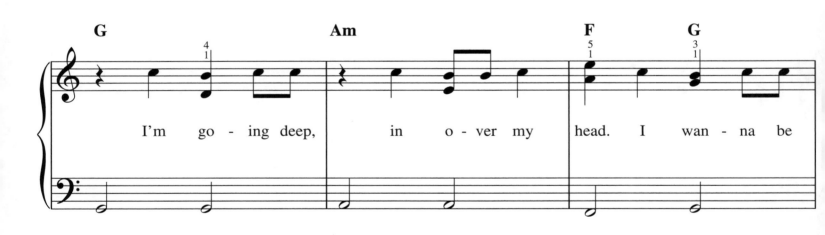

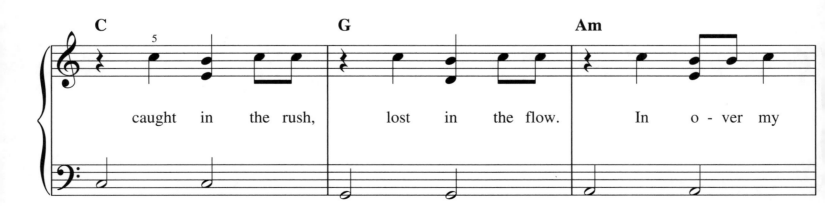

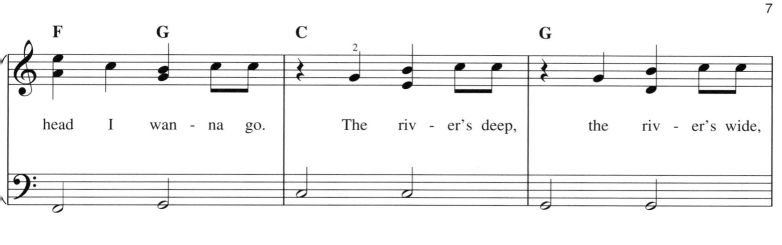

head I wan - na go. The riv - er's deep, the riv - er's wide,

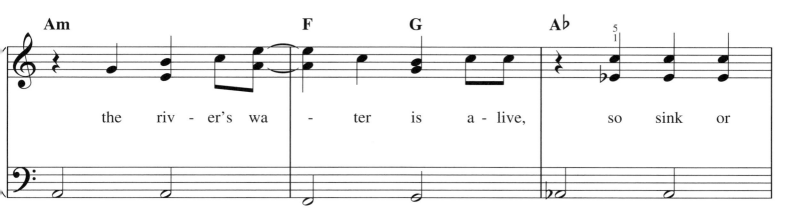

the riv - er's wa - ter is a - live, so sink or

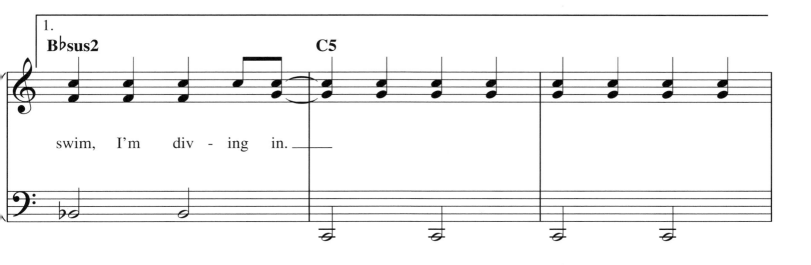

1.

swim, I'm div - ing in.

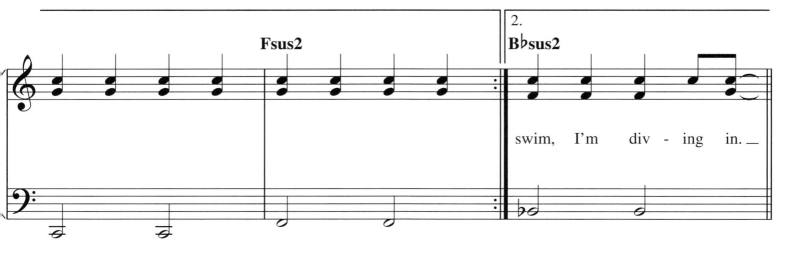

2.

swim, I'm div - ing in.

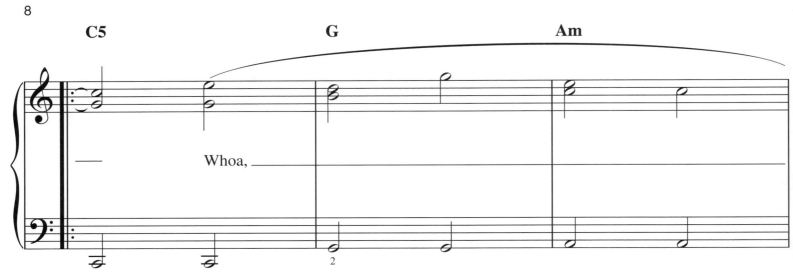

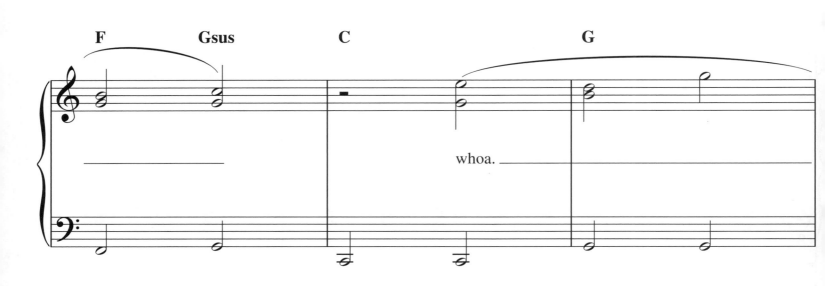

GET DOWN

Words and Music by MARK STUART,
WILL McGINNISS, BOB HERDMAN,
TYLER BURKUM and BEN CISSELL

Moderately fast

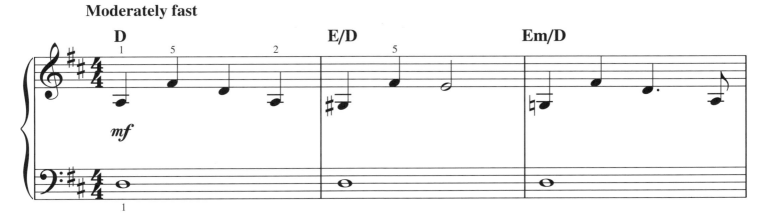

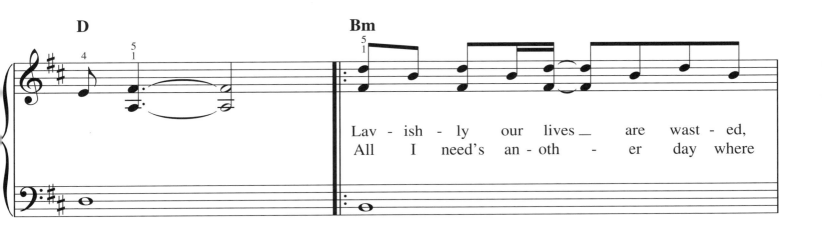

Lav - ish - ly our lives __ are wast - ed,
All I need's an - oth - er day where

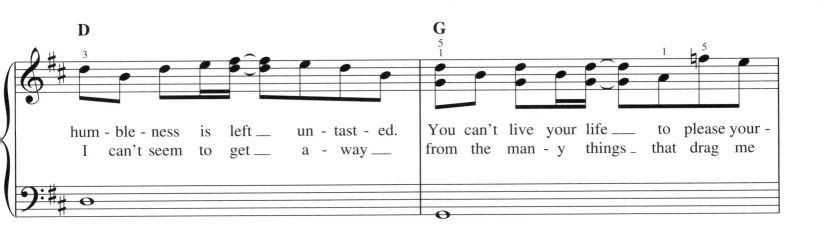

hum - ble - ness is left __ un - tast - ed.
I can't seem to get __ a - way __

You can't live your life __ to please your -
from the man - y things __ that drag me

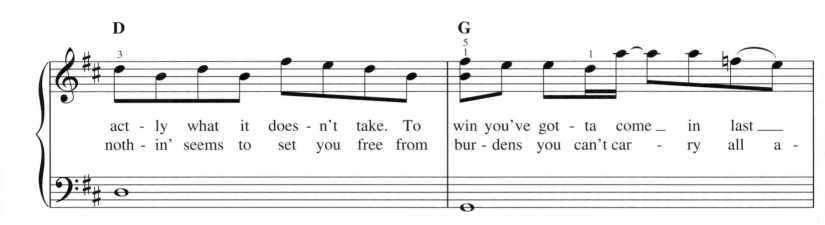

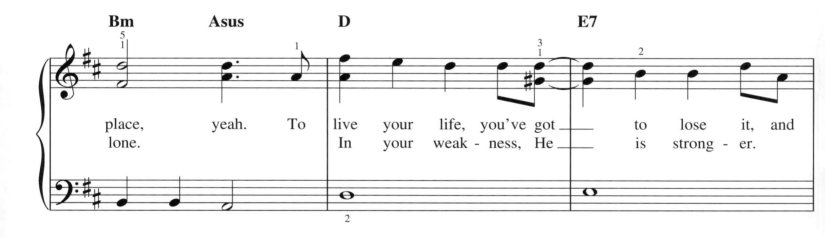

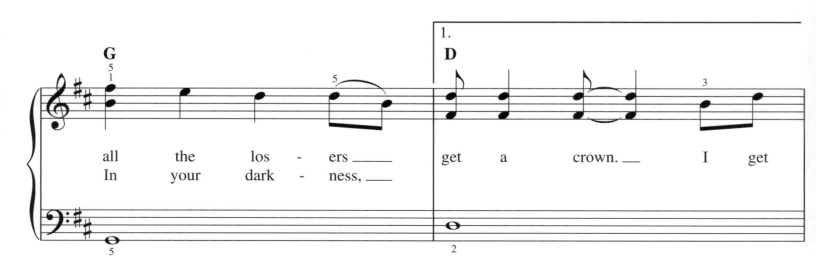

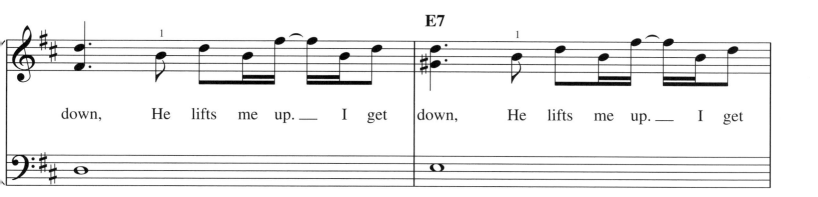

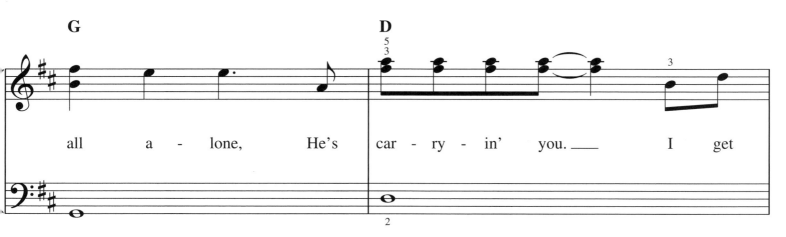

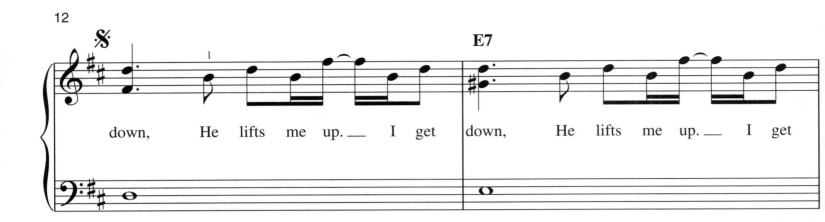

down, He lifts me up. ___ I get down, He lifts me up. ___ I get

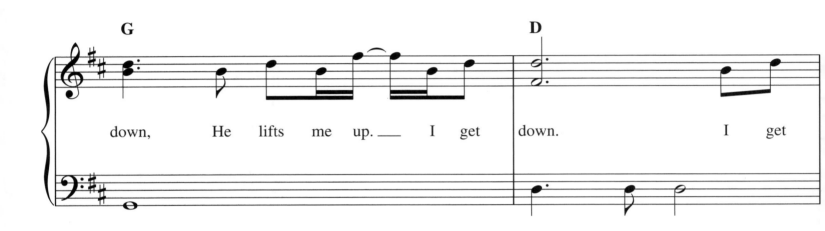

down, He lifts me up. ___ I get down. I get

down, He lifts me up. ___ I get down, He lifts me up. ___ I get

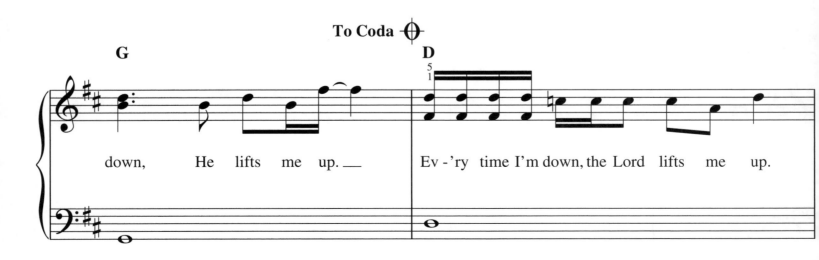

down, He lifts me up. ___ Ev-'ry time I'm down, the Lord lifts me up.

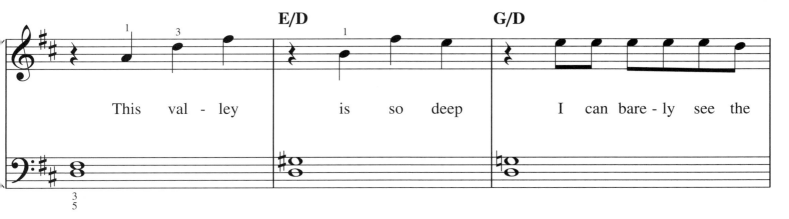

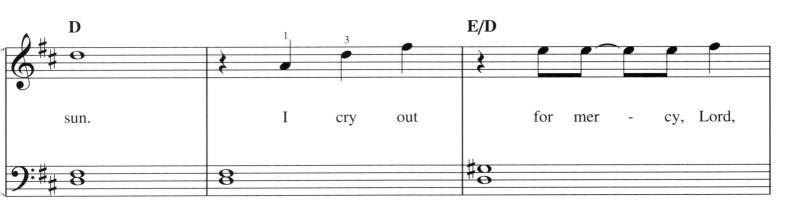

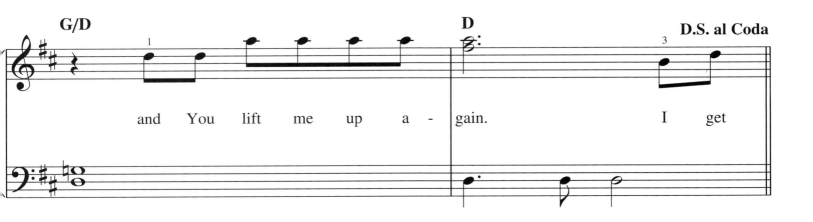

EVERLASTING GOD

Words and Music by BRENTON BROWN
and KEN RILEY

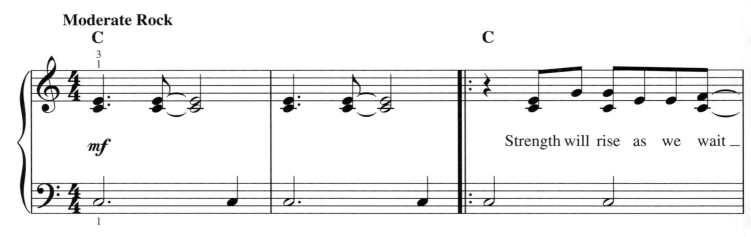

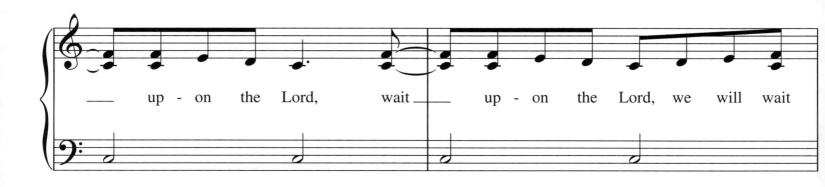

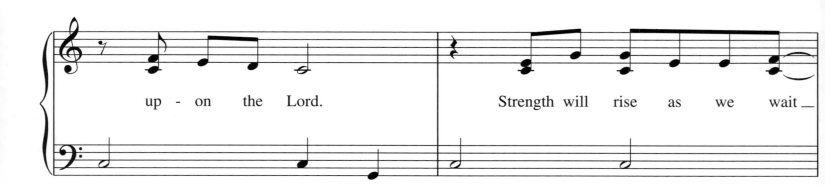

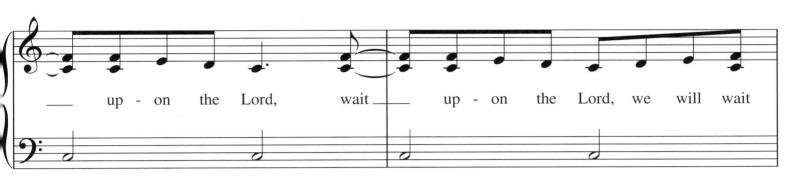

up - on the Lord, wait ____ up - on the Lord, we will wait

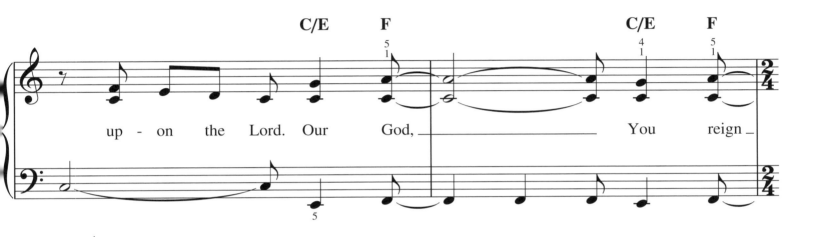

up - on the Lord. Our God, _____ You reign __

__ for - ev _____ er. _____ Our Hope, __

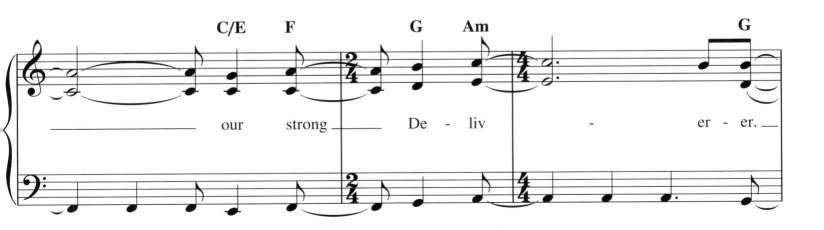

_____ our strong ____ De - liv - er - er. __

16

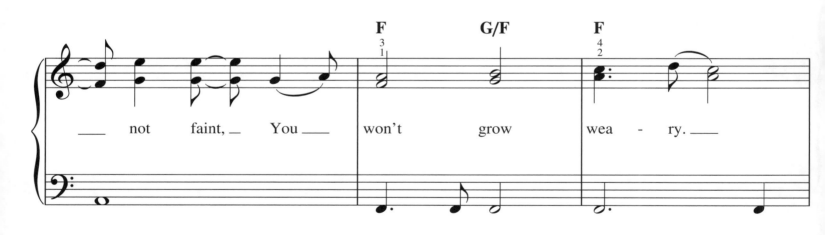

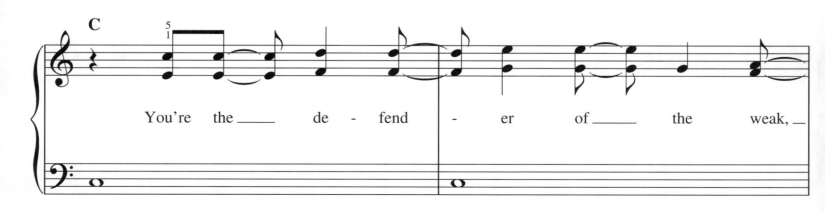

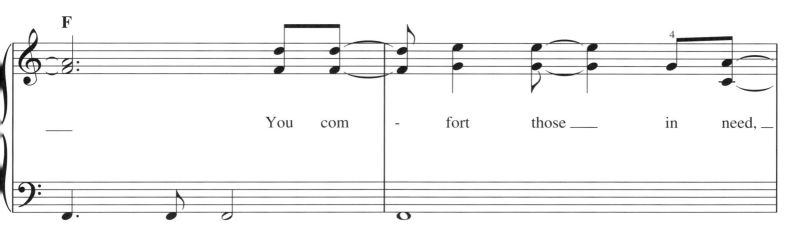

You com - fort those ___ in need, ___

You lift ___ us up ___ on ___ wings like

ea - gles. ___   ea - gles. ___

HOLY

Words and Music by NICHOLE NORDEMAN
and MARK HAMMOND

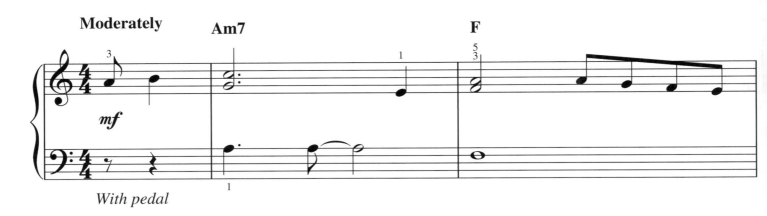

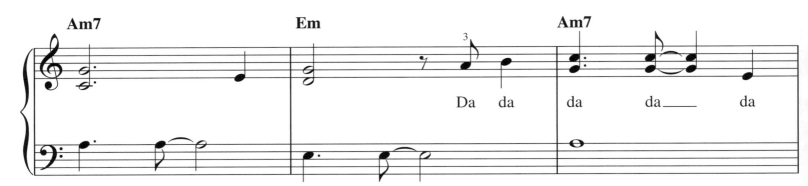

Da da da da da

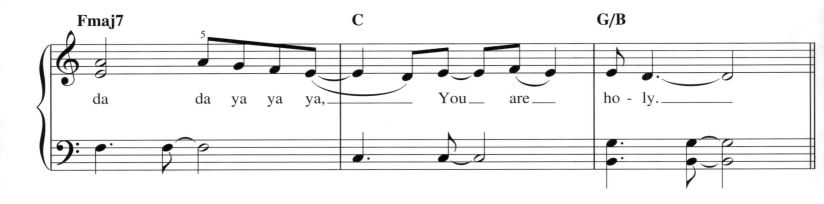

da da ya ya ya, You are ho - ly.

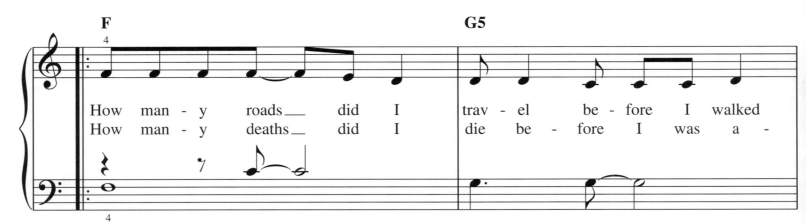

How man - y roads did I trav - el be - fore I walked
How man - y deaths did I die be - fore I was a -

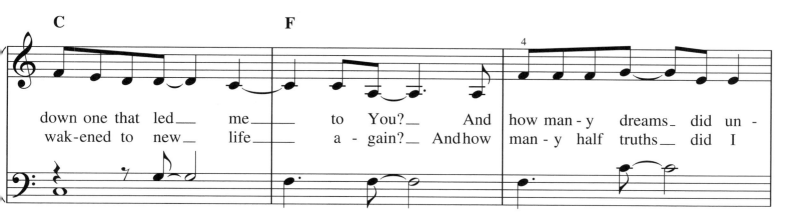

down one that led__ me__ to You?__ And how man - y dreams_ did un -
wak-ened to new_ life__ a - gain?__ And how man - y half truths__ did I

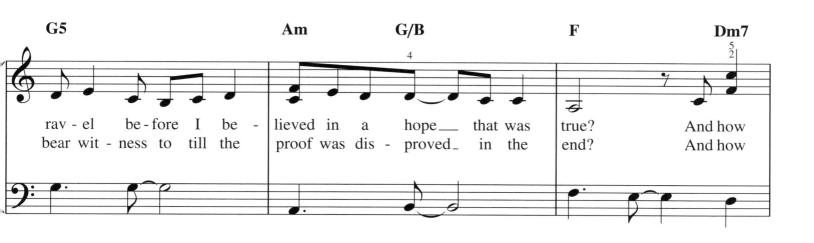

rav - el be - fore I be - lieved in a hope__ that was true? And how
bear wit - ness to till the proof was dis - proved_ in the end? And how

long, how far? What was meant to ful - fill__ on - ly
long, how far? What was meant to il - lu - mi - nate

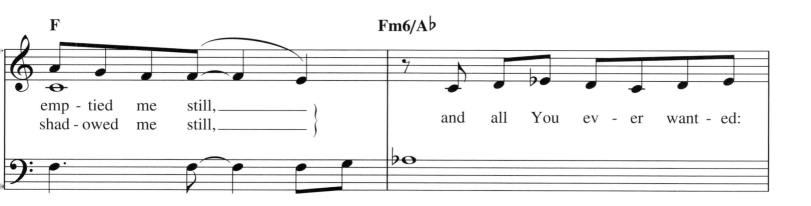

emp - tied me still,_____ and all You ev - er want - ed:
shad - owed me still,_____

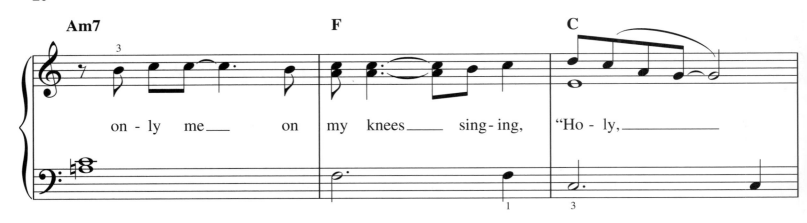

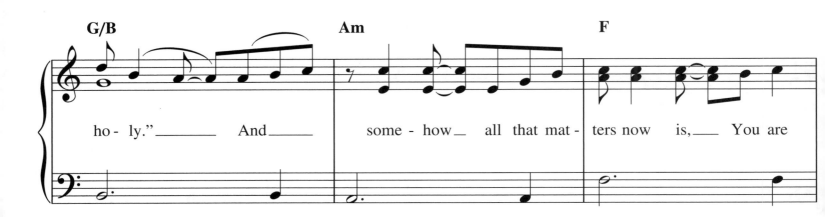

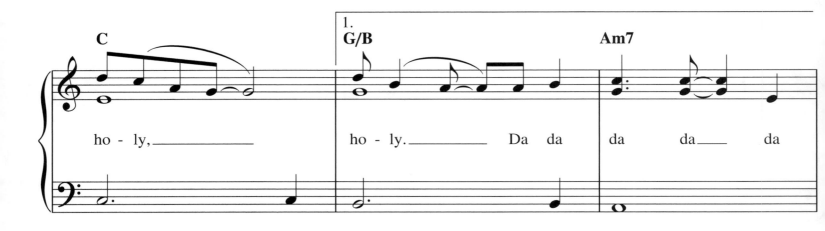

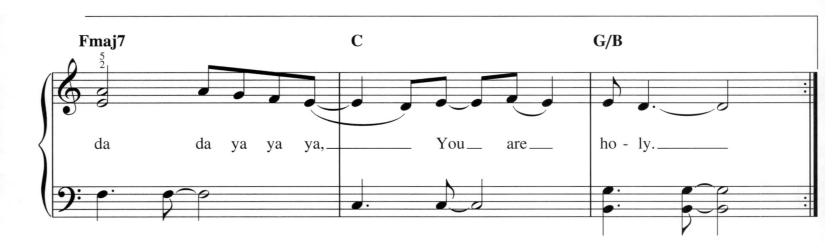

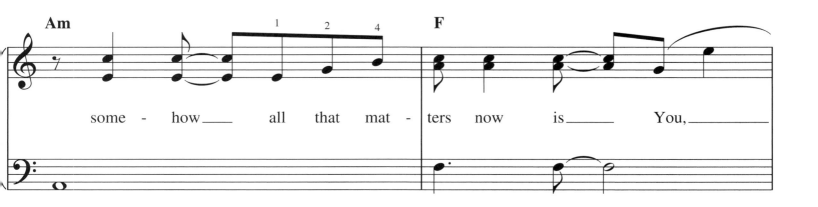

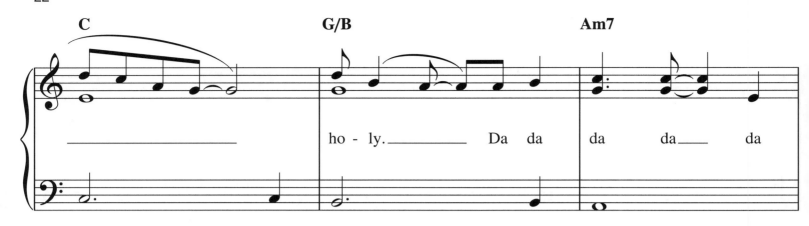

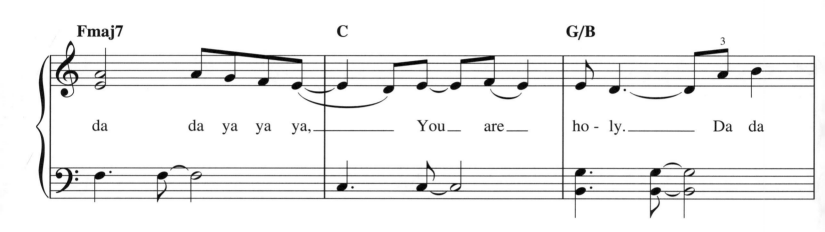

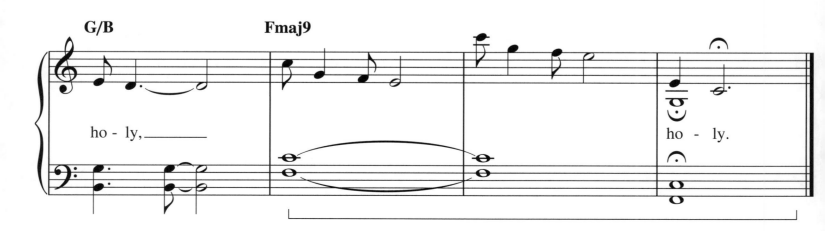

LEARNING TO BREATHE

Words and Music by
JONATHAN FOREMAN

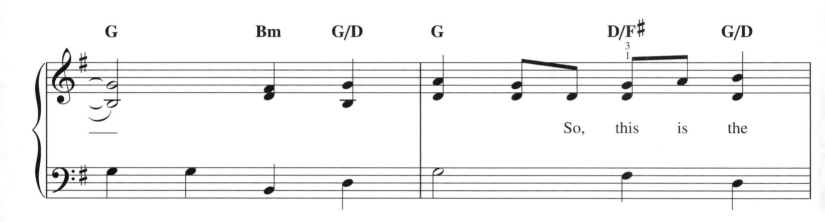

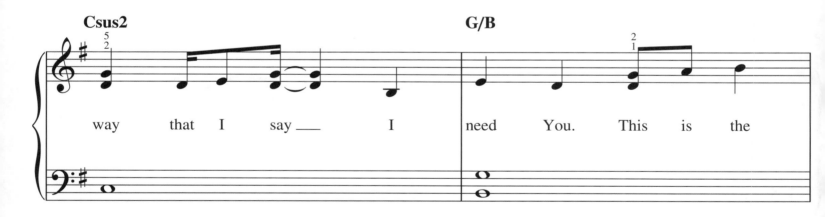

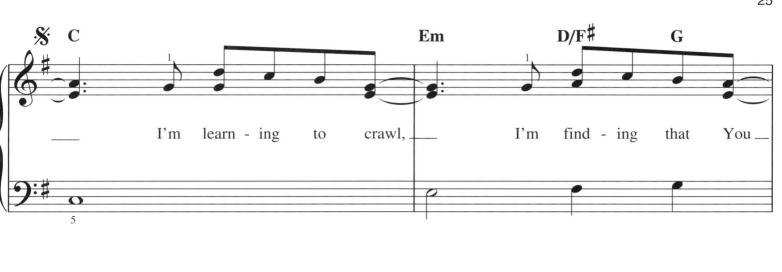

I'm learn - ing to crawl, ___ I'm find - ing that You ___

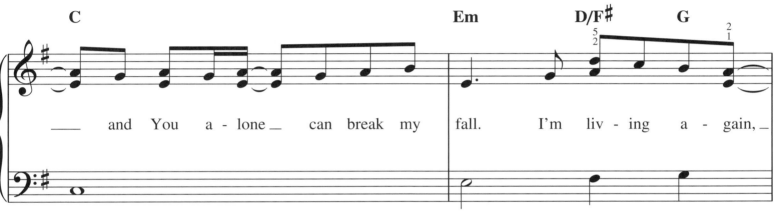

___ and You a - lone ___ can break my fall. I'm liv - ing a - gain, ___

___ a - wake and a - live. ___ I'm dy - ing to breathe ___

To Coda ⊕

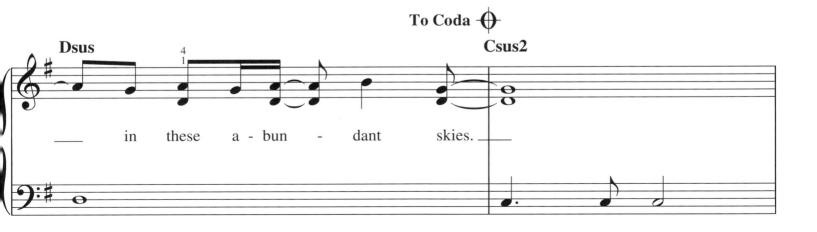

___ in these a - bun - dant skies. ___

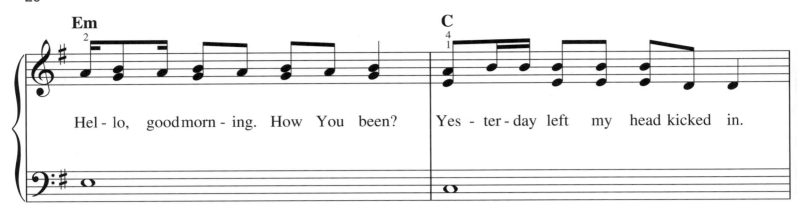

Hel - lo, good morn - ing. How You been? Yes - ter - day left my head kicked in.

I nev - er, nev - er thought that

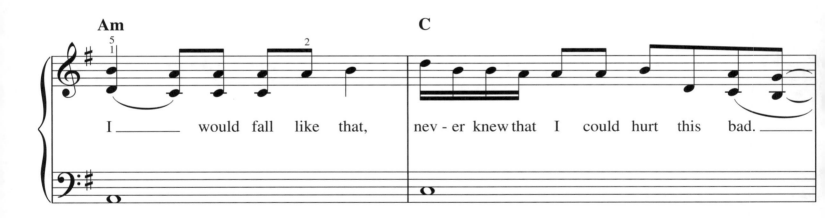

I _____ would fall like that, nev - er knew that I could hurt this bad.

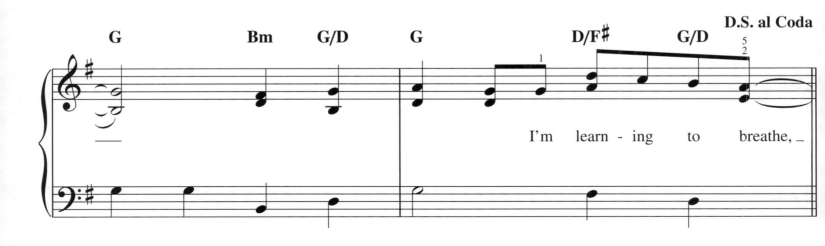

I'm learn - ing to breathe,

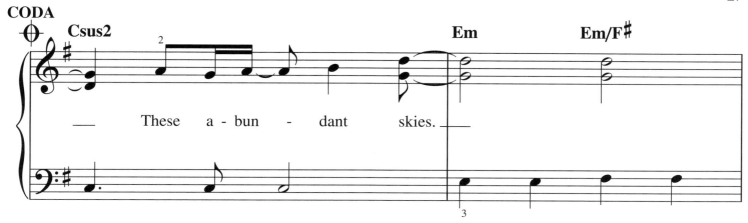

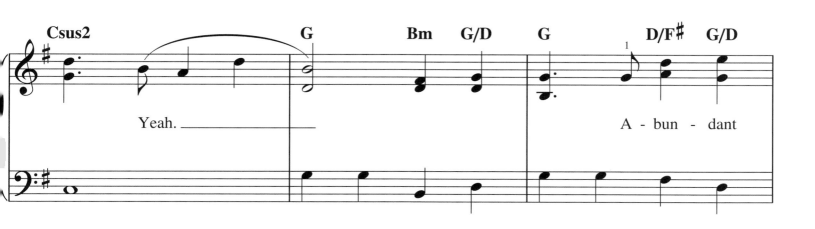

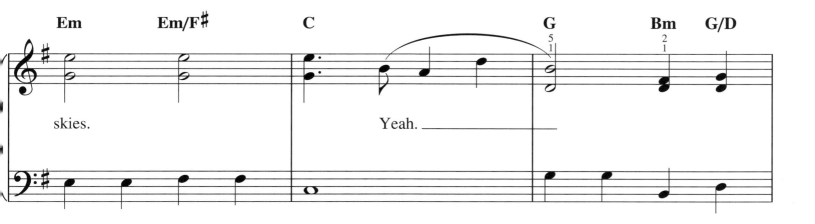

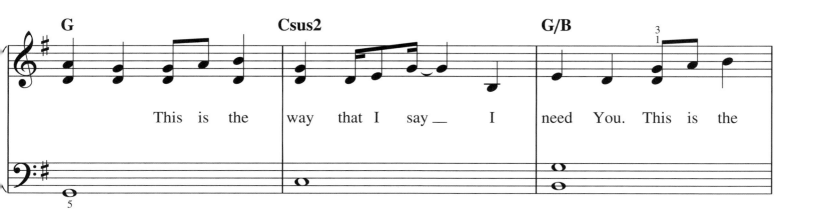

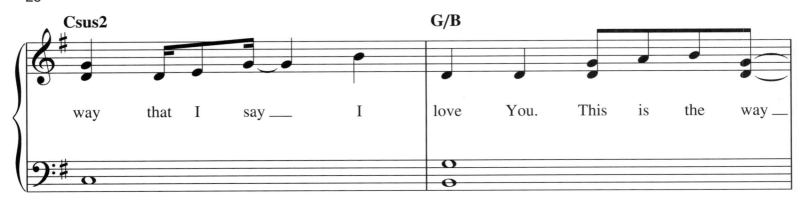

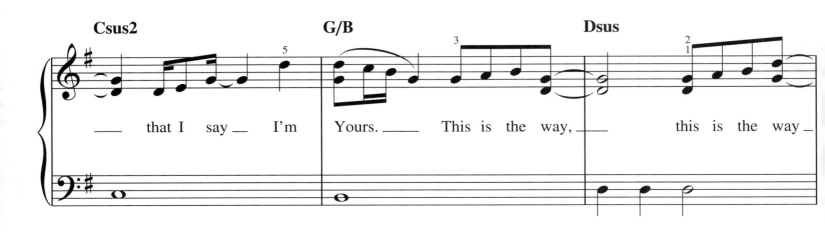

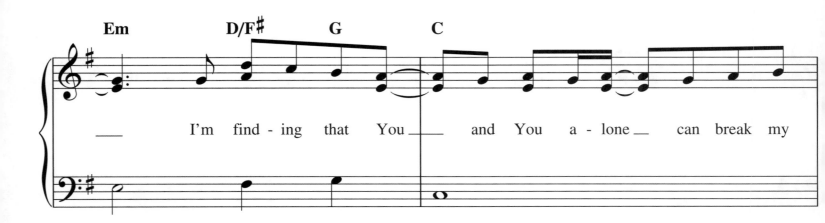

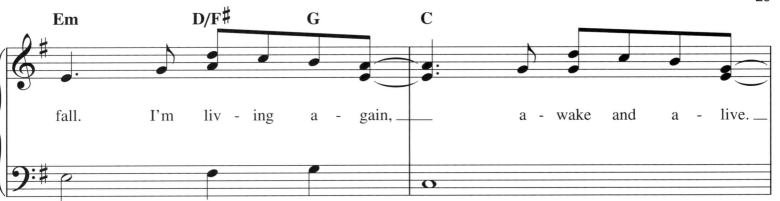

fall. I'm liv - ing a - gain, ___ a - wake and a - live. ___

___ I'm dy - ing to breathe ___ in these a - bun - dant skies. ___

___ Hel - lo, good morn - ing. How You do?

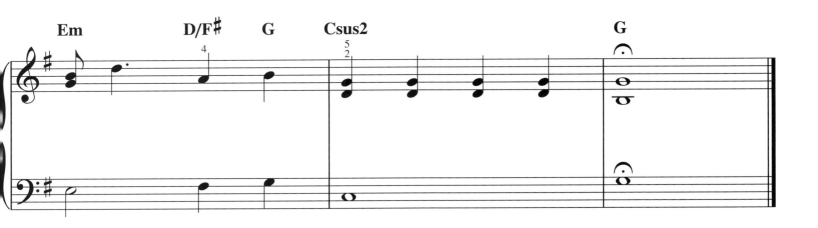

LET IT FADE

Words and Music by JEREMY CAMP
and ADAM WATTS

Have you been

walk - ing on _____ a sur - face that's _____ un -
stand - ing on _____ your own feet _____ too
hold - ing on _____ to what this world _____ has

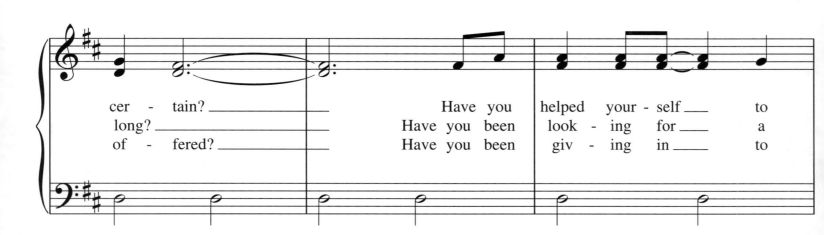

cer - tain? _____ Have you helped your - self _____ to
long? _____ Have you been look - ing for _____ a
of - fered? _____ Have you been giv - ing in _____ to

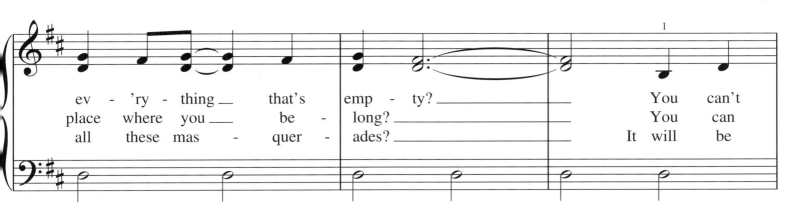

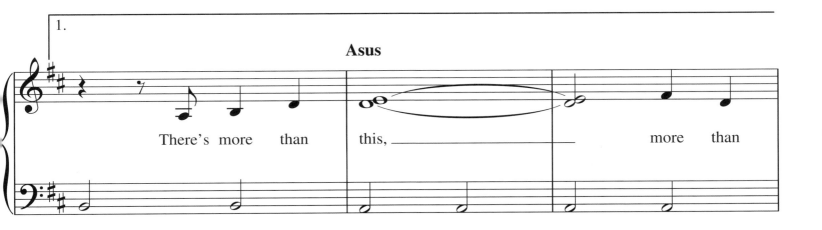

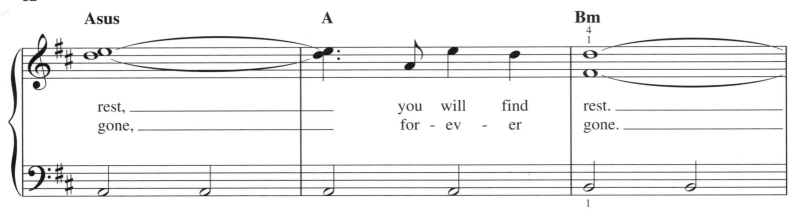

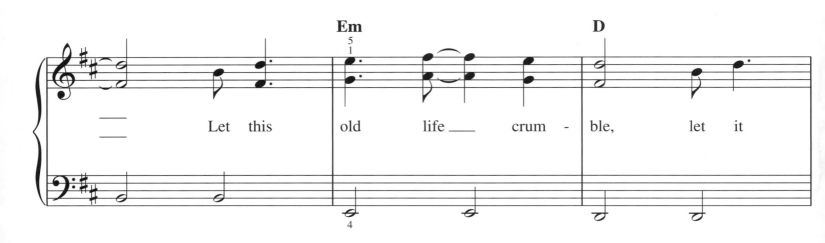

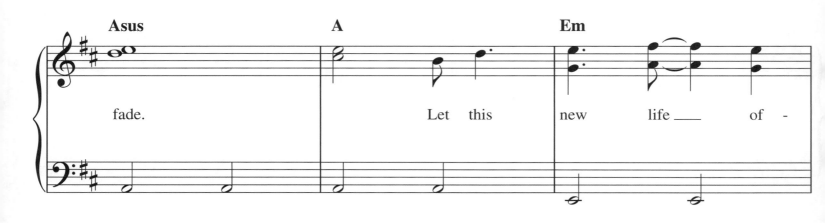

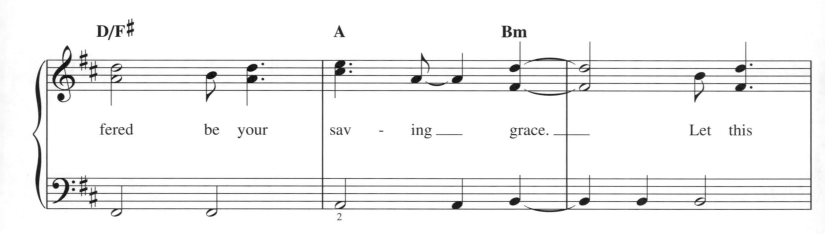

old life ___ crum - ble, let it fade.

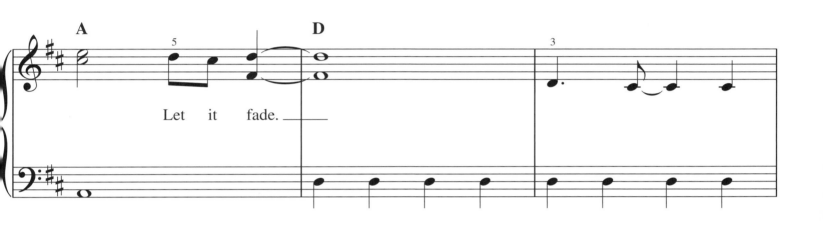

Let it fade. ___

Have you been

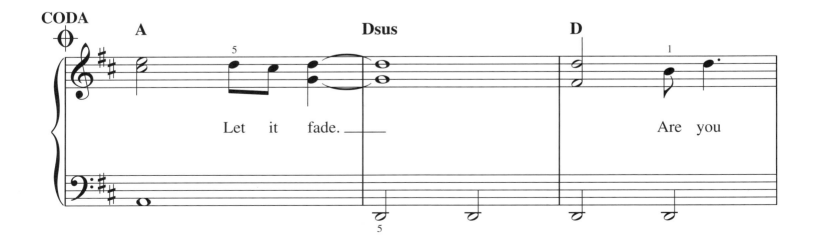

Let it fade. ___ Are you

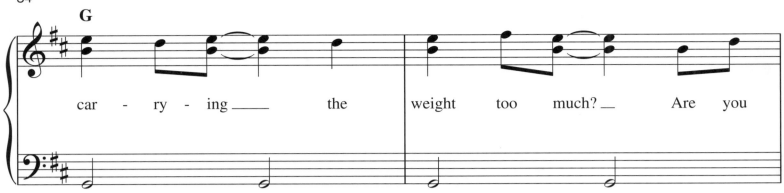

car - ry - ing _____ the weight too much? _ Are you

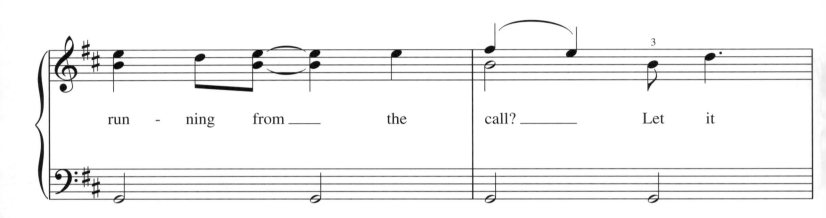

run - ning from _____ the call? _____ Let it

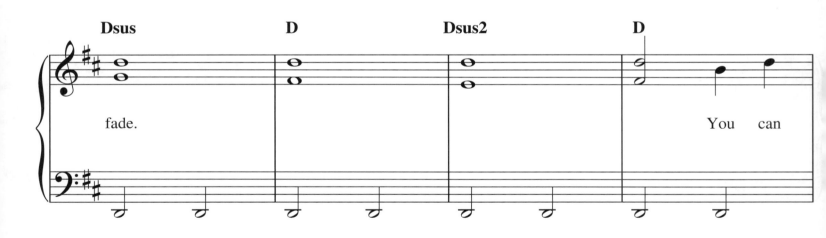

fade. You can

rest, _____ you will find rest. _____

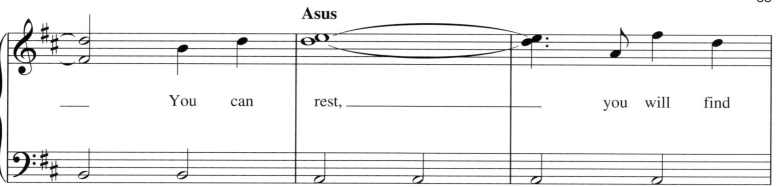

You can rest, you will find

rest. Let this old life crum-

ble, let it fade. Let this

new life of - fered be your sav - ing grace.

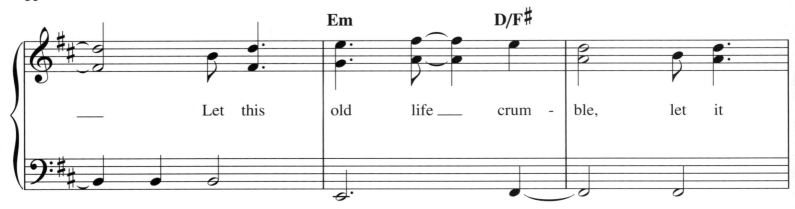

Let this old life ___ crum - ble, let it

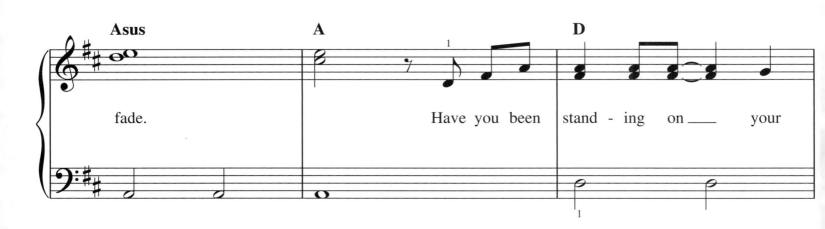

fade. Have you been stand - ing on ___ your

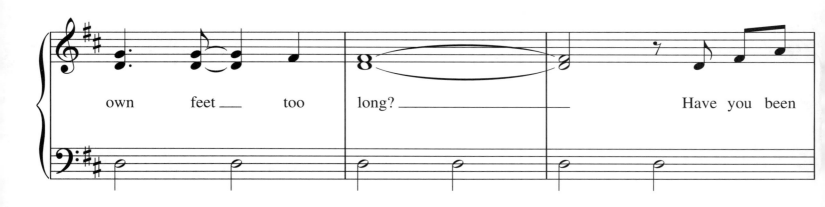

own feet ___ too long? ___ Have you been

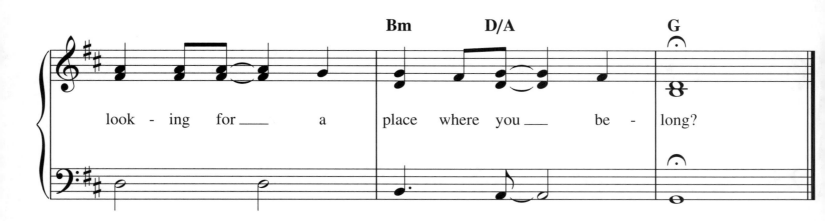

look - ing for ___ a place where you ___ be - long?

REVELATION

Words by MAC POWELL
Music by THIRD DAY

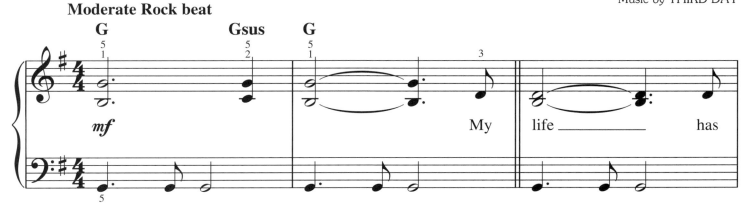

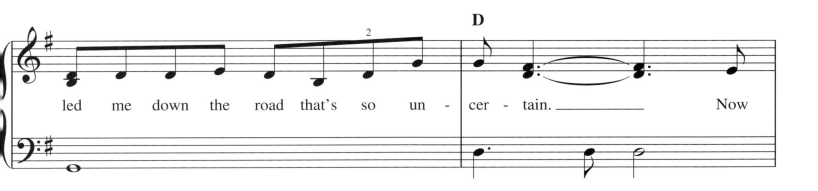

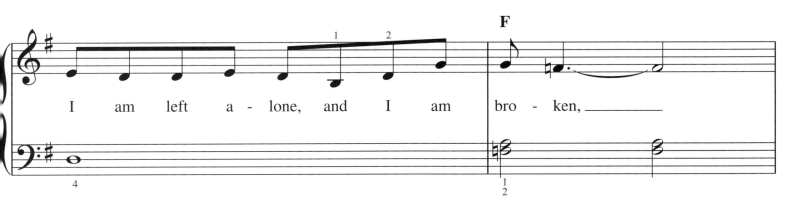

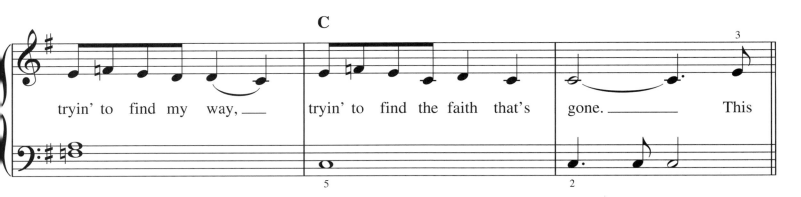

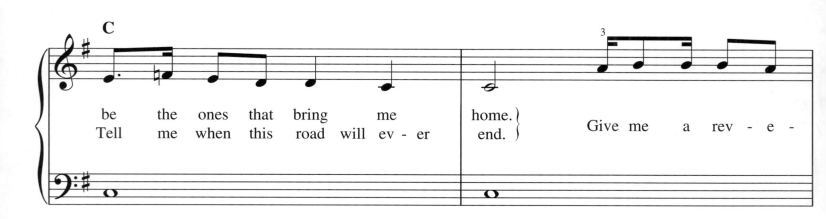

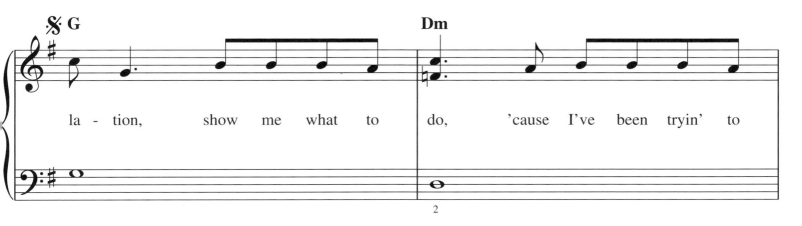

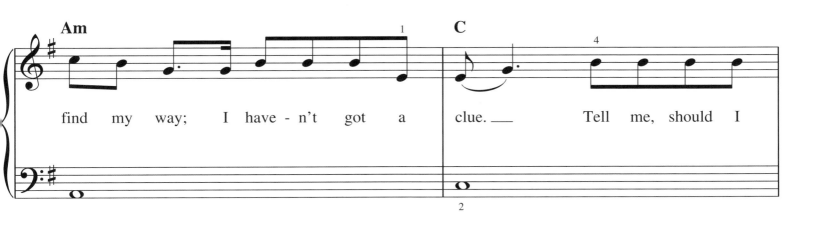

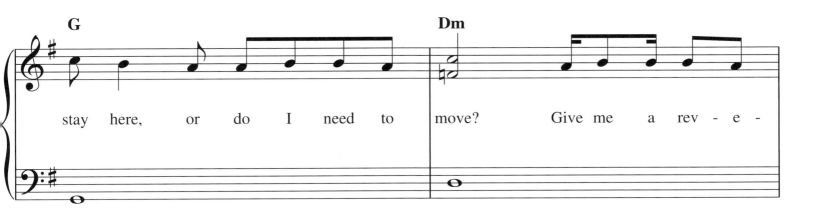

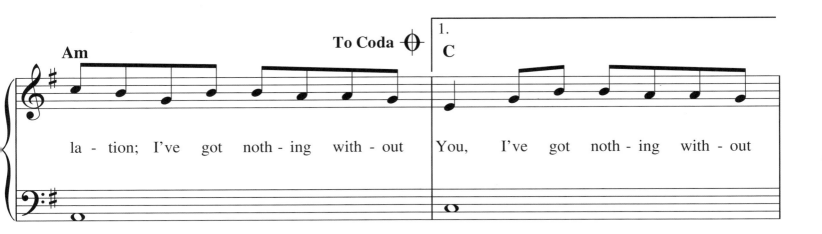

40

You. My

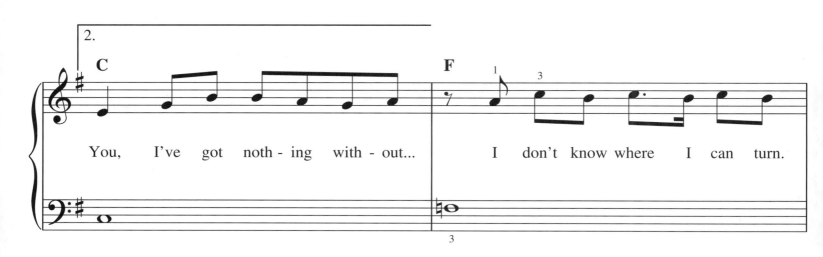

You, I've got noth - ing with - out... I don't know where I can turn.

Tell me, when will I learn? Won't You show me where I need to

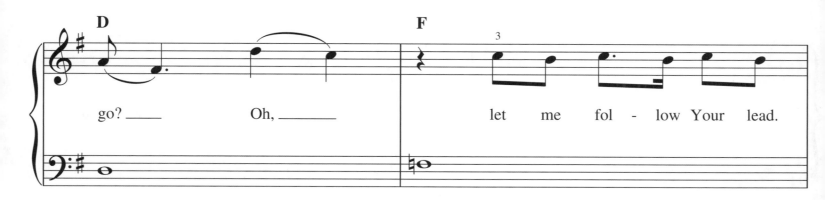

go? ___ Oh, ___ let me fol - low Your lead.

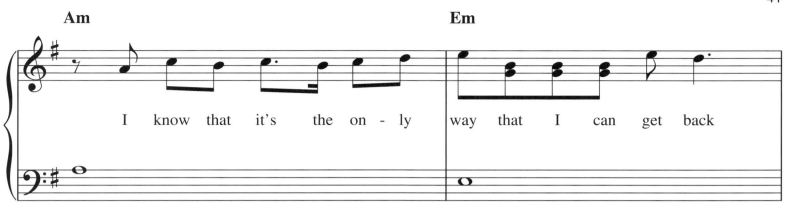

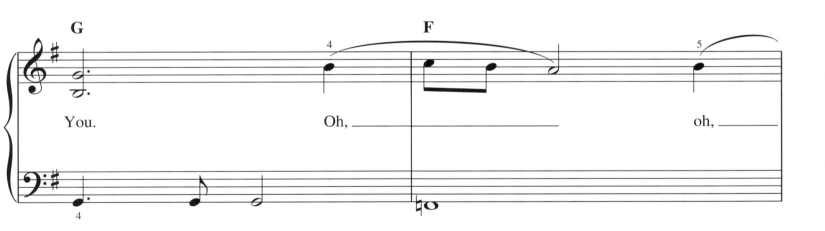

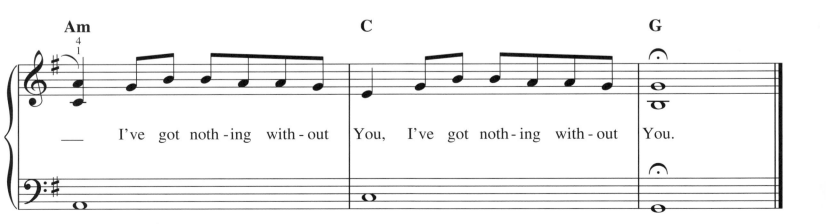

MADE TO LOVE

Words and Music by TOBY McKEEHAN,
CARY BARLOWE, JAMIE MOORE
and AARON RICE

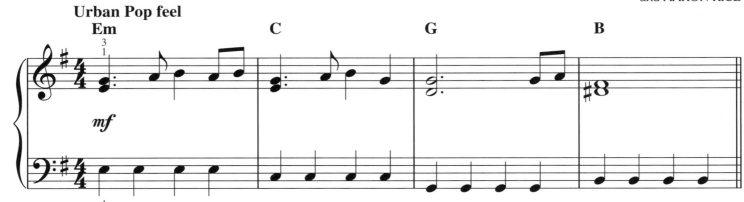

The dream is fad-ing, now I'm star-ing at the door. I know it's o-ver 'cause my feet have hit the cold floor.

Check my re-flec-tion, I ain't feel-in' what I see. It's no mys-ter-y.

What-ev-er hap-pened to a pas-sion I could live for? What be-came of the flame that made me feel more?

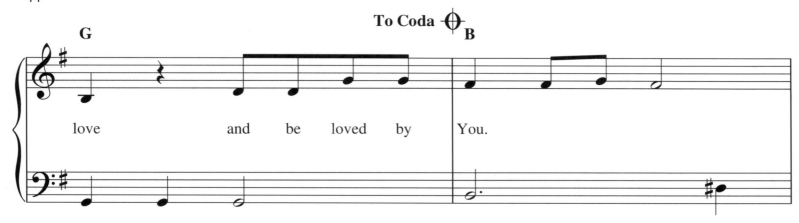

To Coda

love and be loved by You.

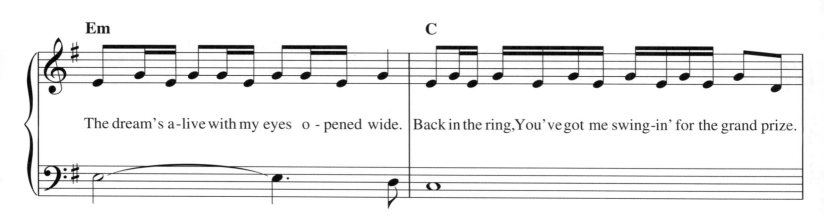

The dream's a-live with my eyes o-pened wide. Back in the ring, You've got me swing-in' for the grand prize.

I feel the hate is spit-tin' va-pors on my dreams, but I still be-lieve.

I'm reach-in' out, reach-in' up, reach-in' o-ver, I feel a breeze cov-er me called "Je-ho-vah."

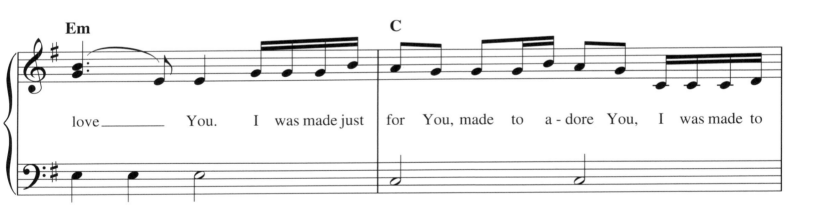

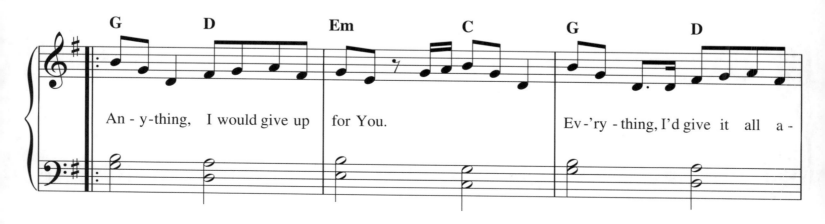

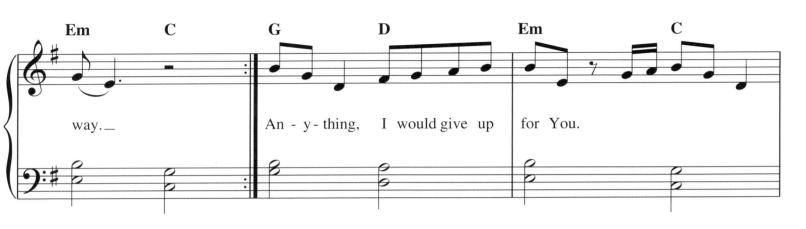

ONLY GRACE

Words and Music by KENNETH GREENBERG
and MATTHEW WEST

Pop Ballad

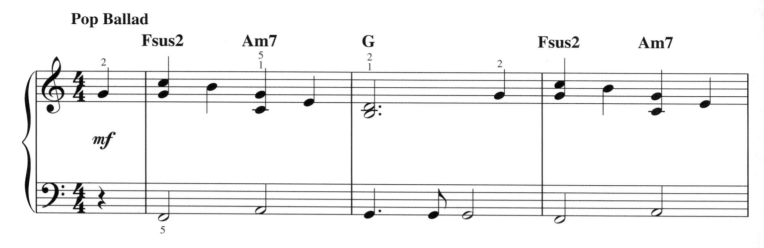

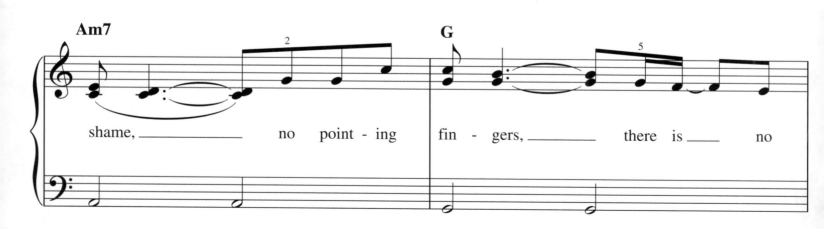

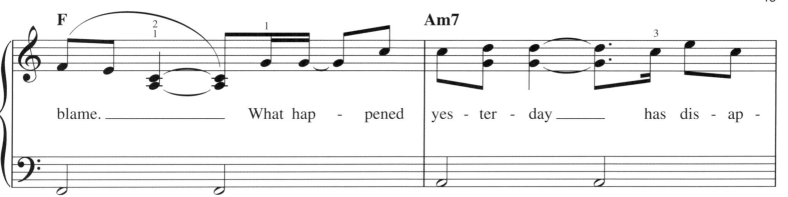

blame._____ What hap - pened yes - ter - day ___ has dis - ap -

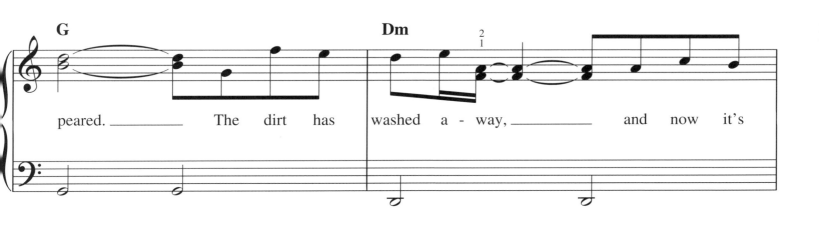

peared. _____ The dirt has washed a - way, _____ and now it's

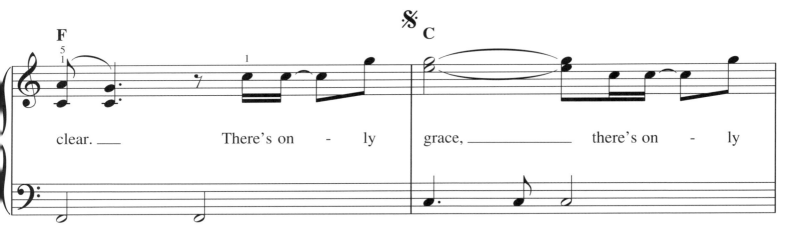

clear. ___ There's on - ly grace, _____ there's on - ly

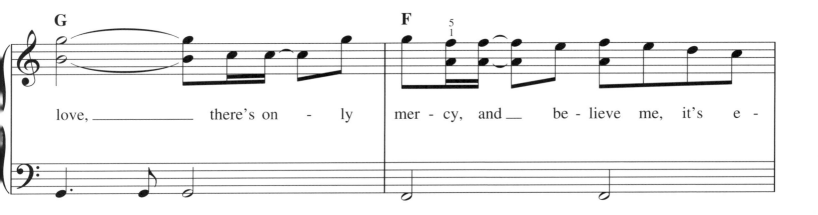

love, _____ there's on - ly mer - cy, and __ be - lieve me, it's e -

50

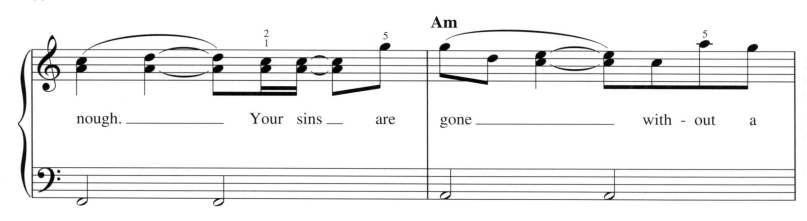

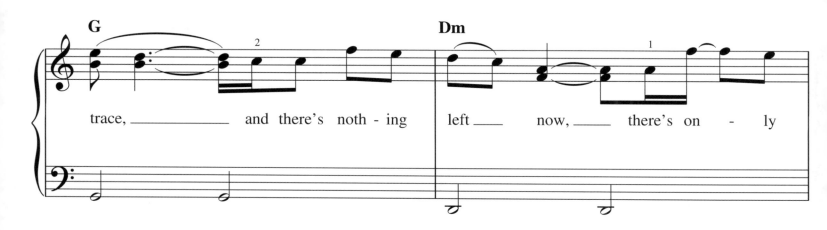

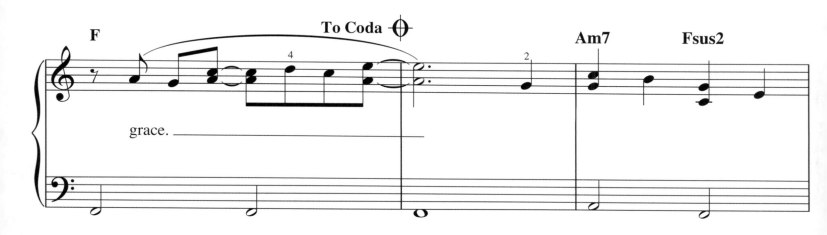

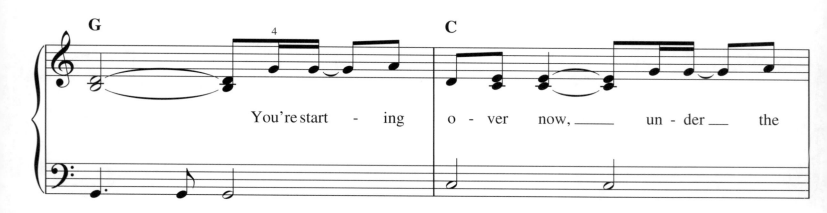

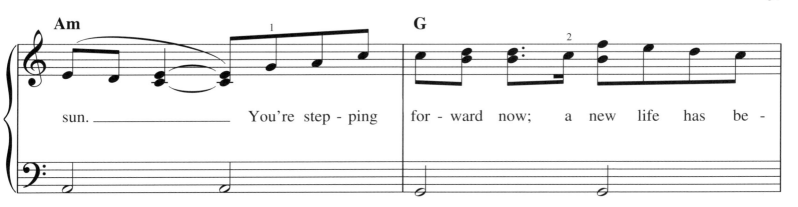

sun. _____ You're step - ping for - ward now; a new life has be -

gun. Your new life has be - gun. _____ There's on - ly

_____ And if you should fall a - gain, ___ well, get back

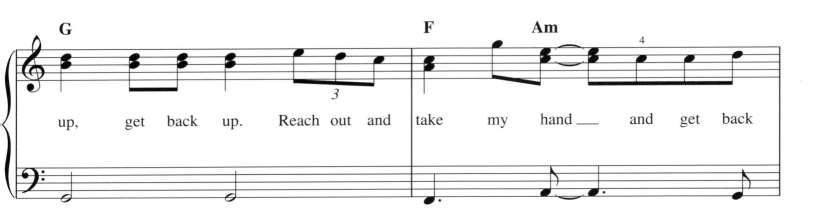

up, get back up. Reach out and take my hand ___ and get back

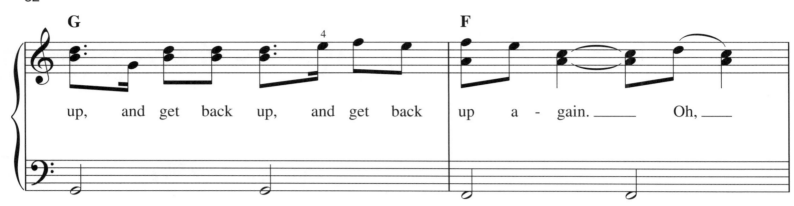

up, and get back up, and get back up a - gain. _____ Oh, _____

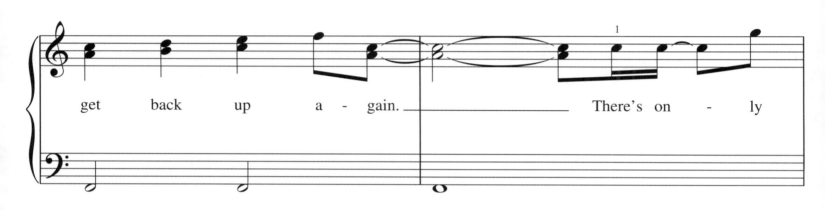

get back up a - gain. _____ There's on - ly

grace, _____ there's on - ly love, _____ there's on - ly

mer - cy, and _ be - lieve me, it's e - nough. _____ Your sins _ are

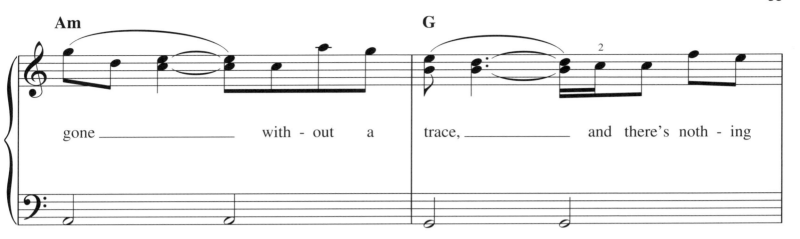

gone _____ with - out a trace, _____ and there's noth - ing

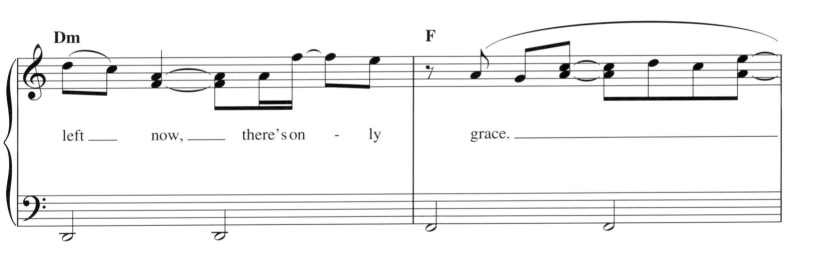

left ___ now, ___ there's on - ly grace. _____

SEA OF FACES

Words and Music by JON MICAH SUMRALL,
KYLE MITCHELL, JAMES MEAD,
RYAN SHROUT and AARON SPRINKLE

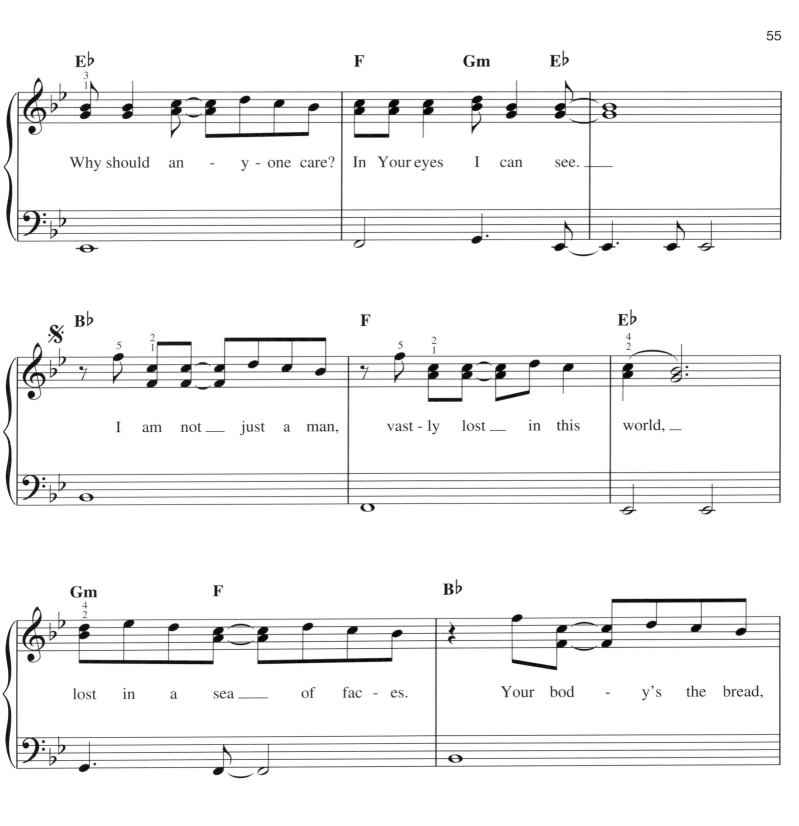

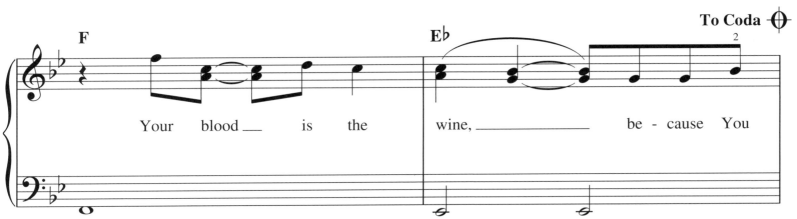

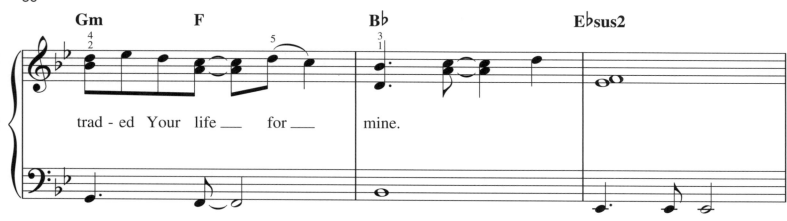

trad - ed Your life ___ for ___ mine.

Some - times _ my

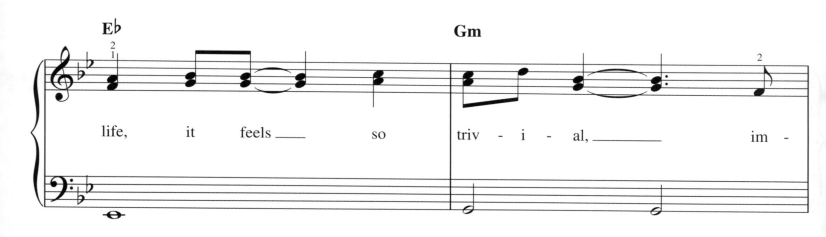

life, it feels ____ so triv - i - al, _____ im -

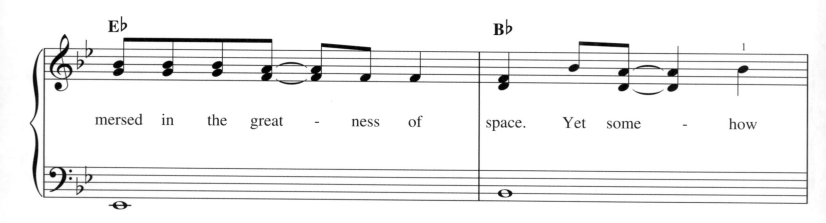

mersed in the great - ness of space. Yet some - how

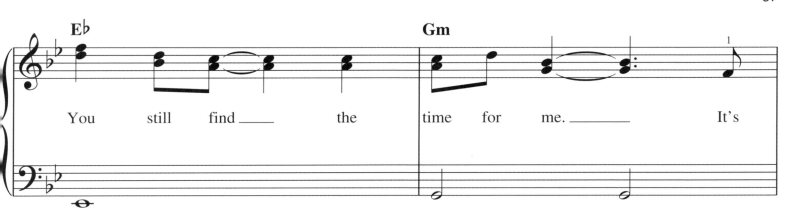

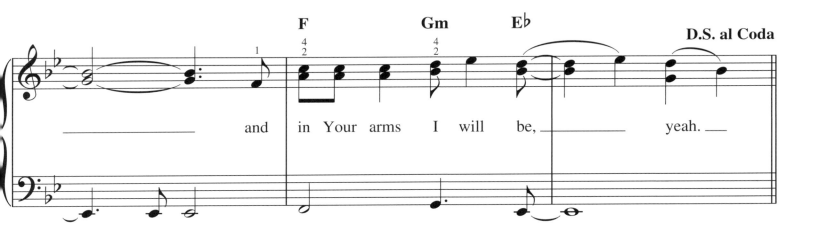

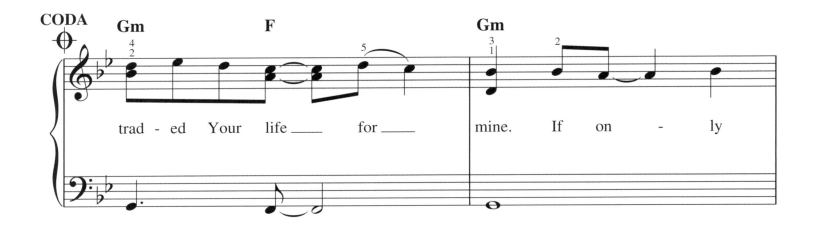

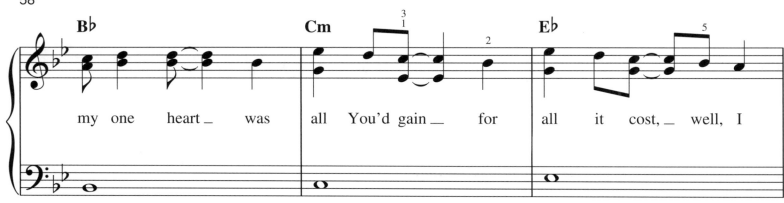

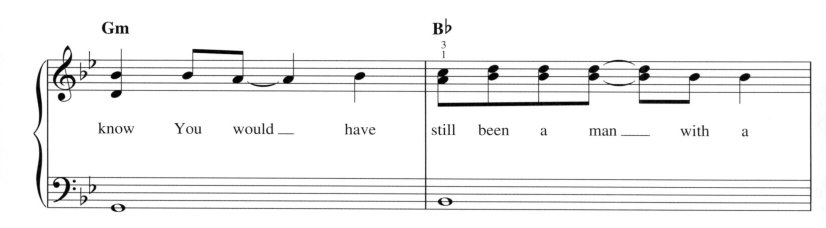

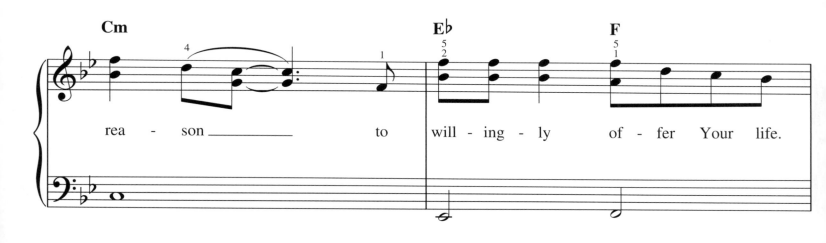

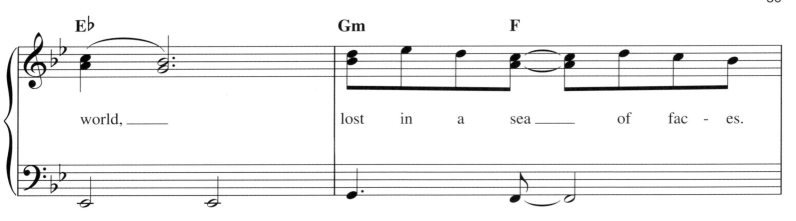

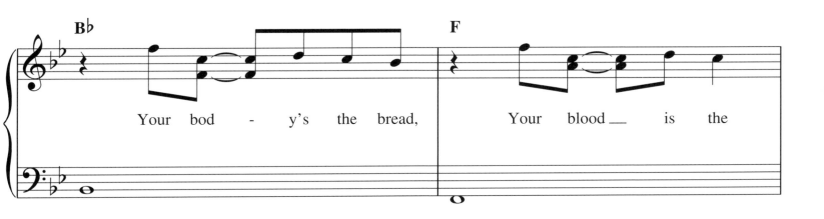

SHINE

Words and Music by PETER FURLER
and STEVE TAYLOR

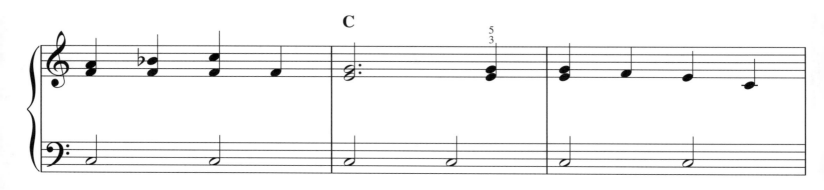

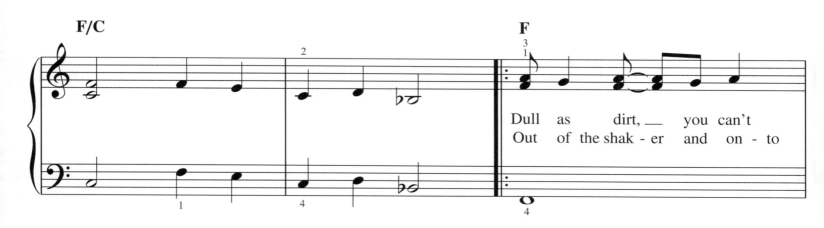

Dull as dirt, __ you can't
Out of the shak - er and on - to

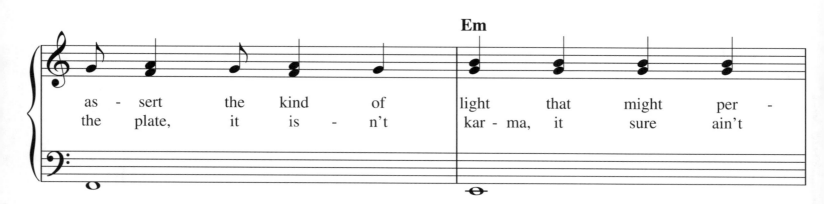

as - sert the kind of light that might per -
the plate, it is - n't kar - ma, it might sure ain't

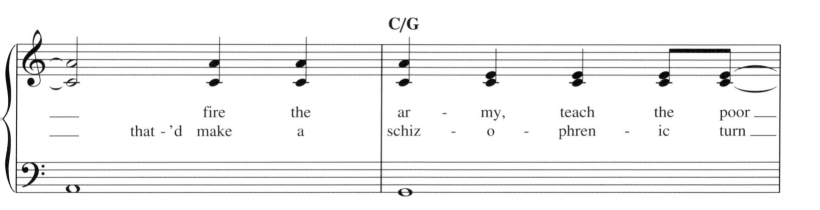

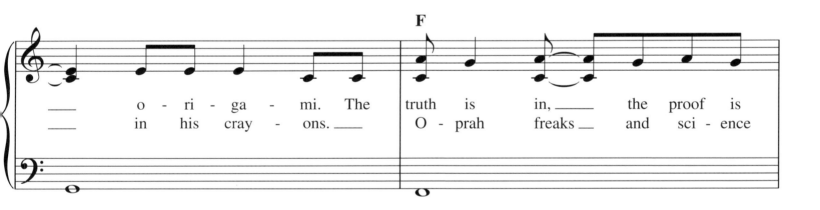

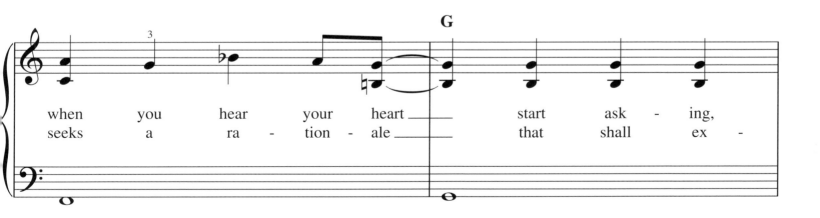

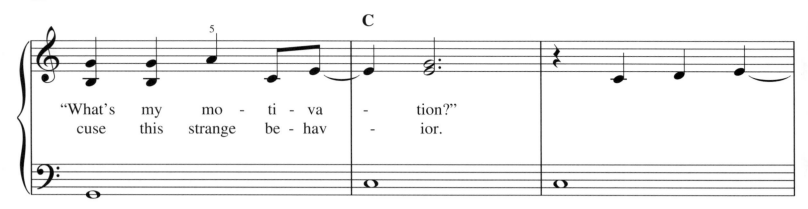

C

"What's my mo - ti - va - tion?"
cuse this strange be - hav - ior.

F

And try as you may, __ there is - n't
When you let it ___ shine, __ you will in -

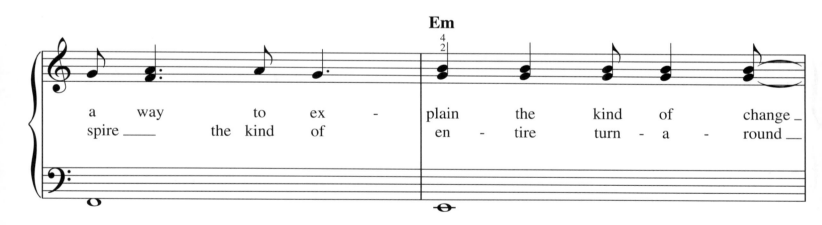

Em

a way to ex - plain the kind of change __
spire ___ the kind of en - tire turn - a - round __

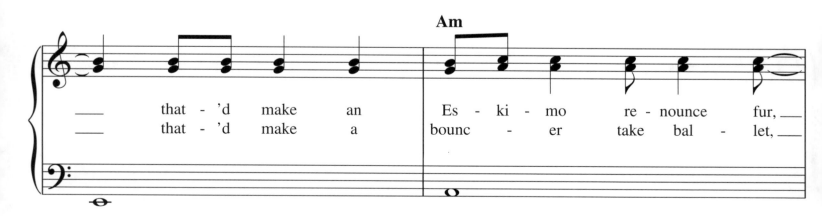

Am

__ that - 'd make an Es - ki - mo re - nounce fur, __
__ that - 'd make a bounc - er take bal - let, __

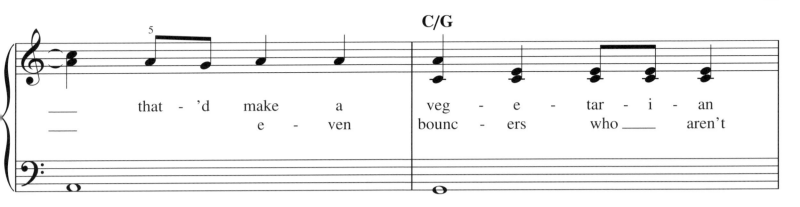

that – 'd make a veg – e – tar – i – an
e – ven bounc – ers who _____ aren't

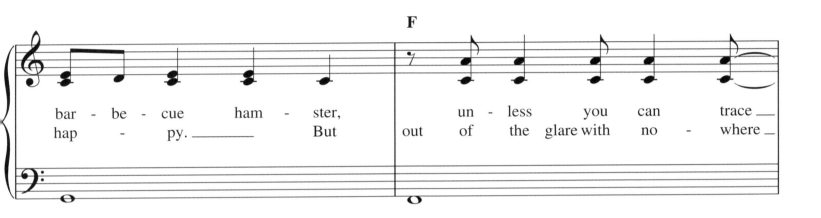

bar – be – cue ham – ster, un – less you can trace _____
hap – py. _____ But out of the glare with no – where _____

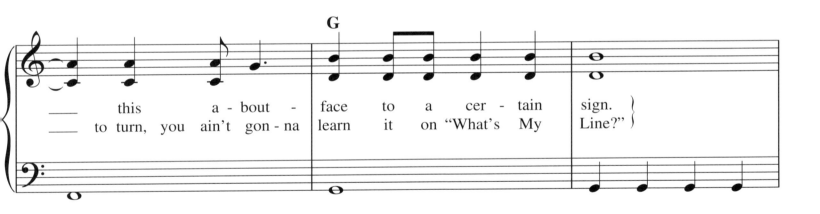

_____ this a – bout – face to a cer – tain sign.
_____ to turn, you ain't gon – na learn it on "What's My Line?"

Shine. Make 'em won – der what you've got. _____ Make 'em

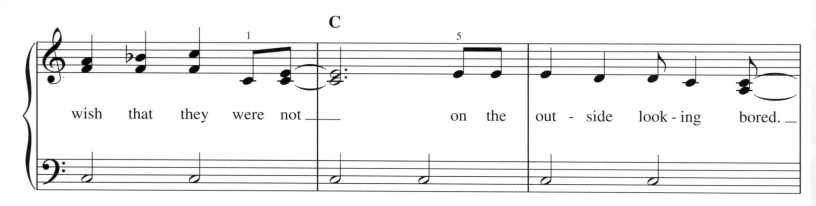

wish that they were not ___ on the out-side look-ing bored. ___

___ Shine. Let it

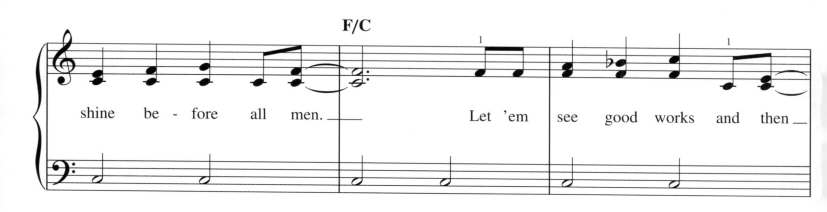

shine be - fore all men. ___ Let 'em see good works and then ___

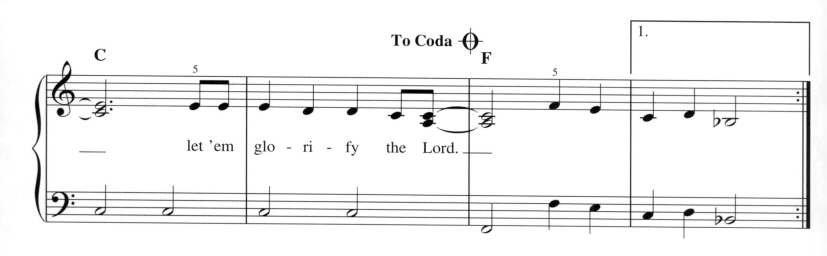

To Coda ⊕

1.

___ let 'em glo-ri-fy the Lord. ___

SONG OF LOVE

Words and Music by REBECCA ST. JAMES,
MATT BRONLEEWE and JEREMY ASH

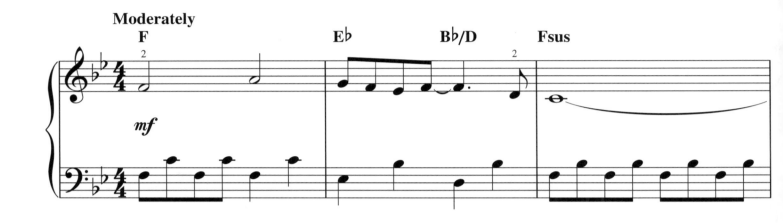

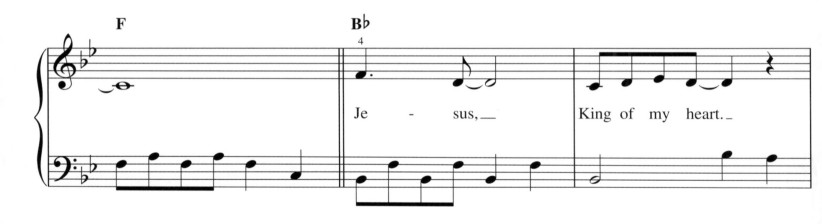

Je - sus,___ King of my heart.___

Fa - ther,___ my peace and my light.___ Spir - it,___ the

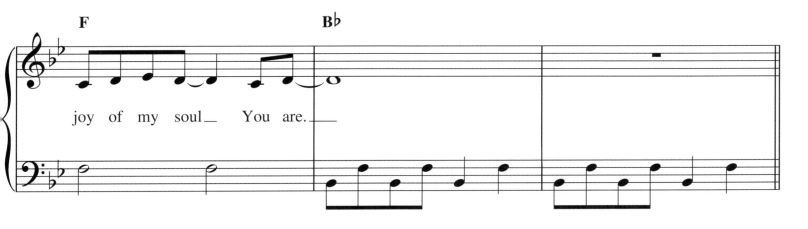

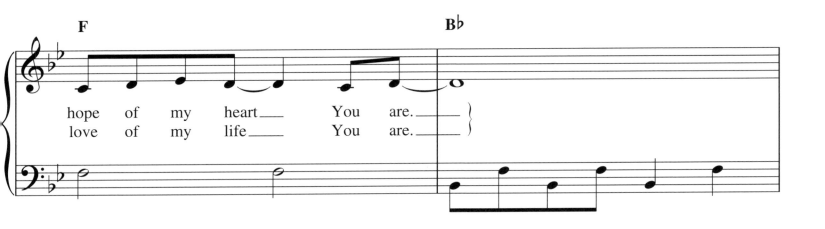

68

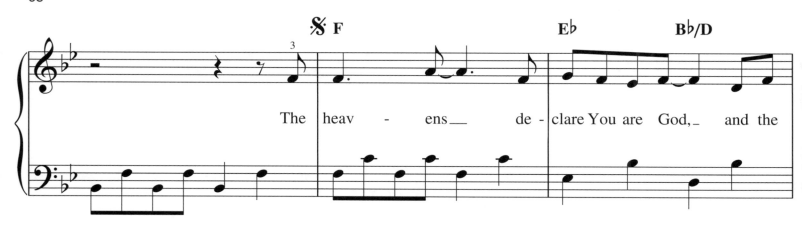

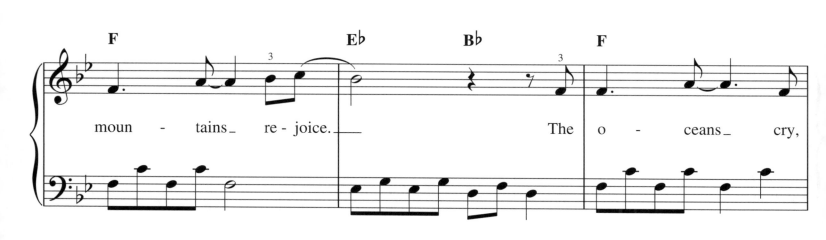

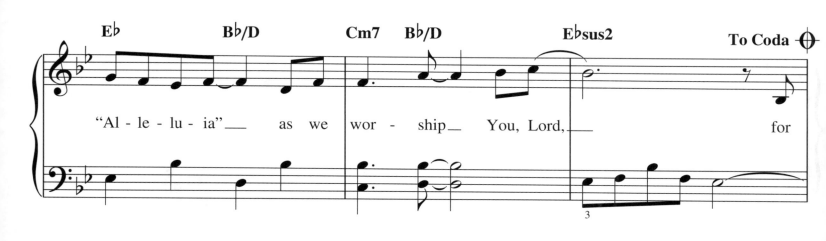

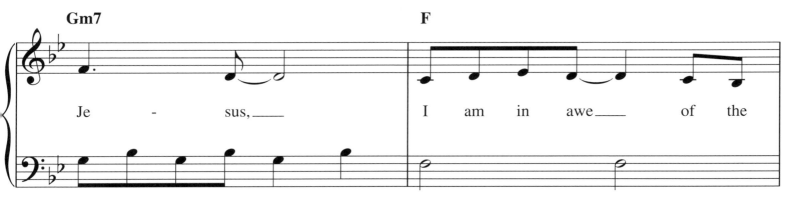

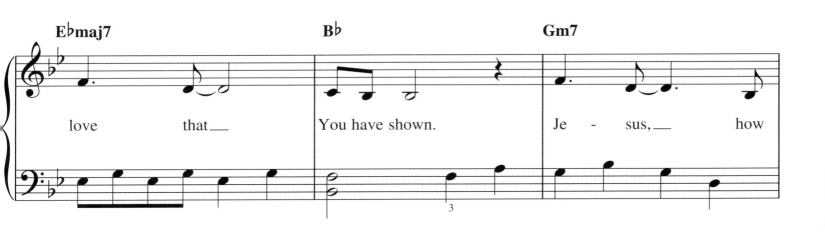

YOU ARE THE ANSWER

Words and Music by MATT HUESMANN
and REGIE HAMM

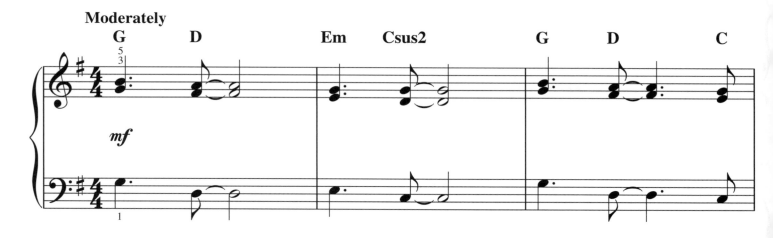

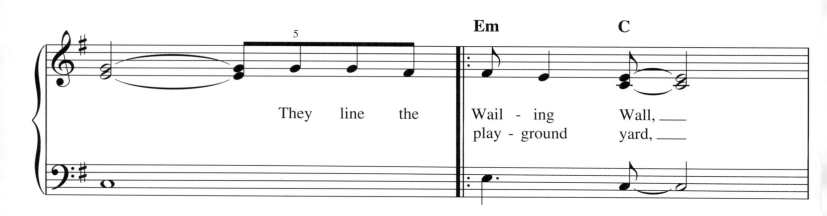

They line the

Wail - ing Wall, ___
play - ground yard, ___

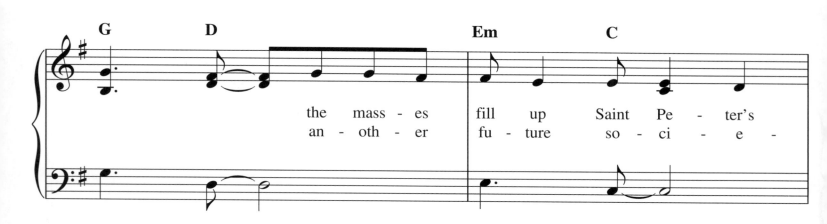

the mass - es
an - oth - er

fill up Saint Pe - ter's
fu - ture so - ci - e -

71

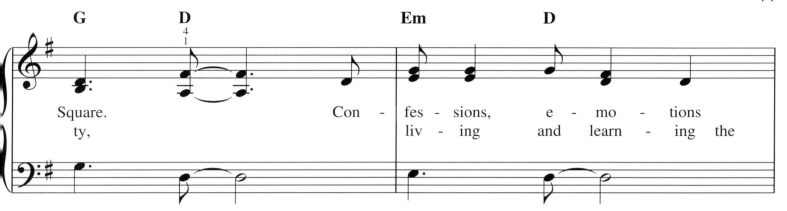

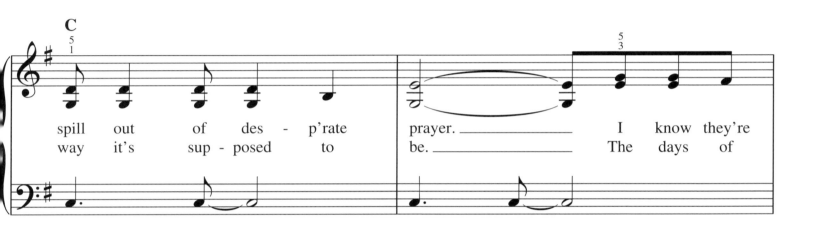

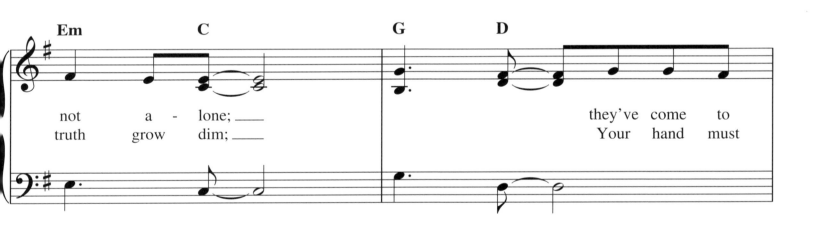

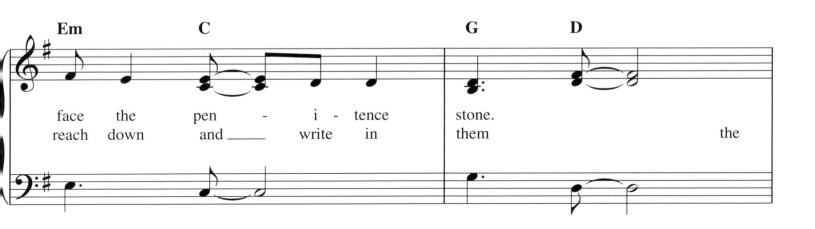

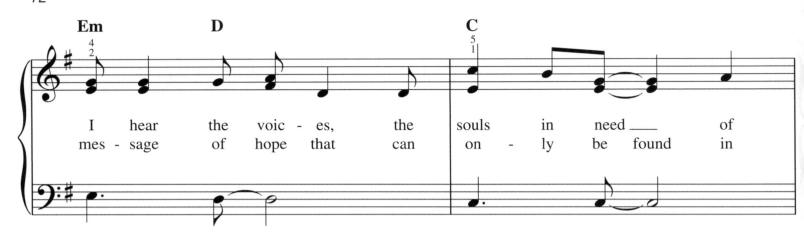

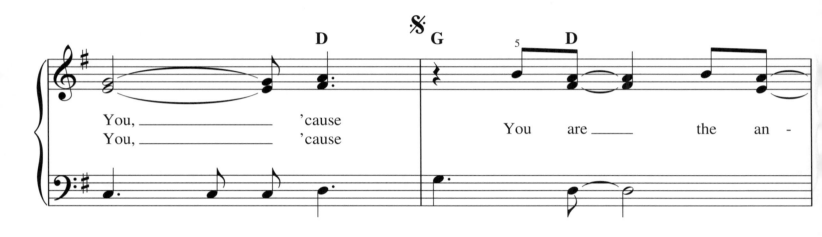

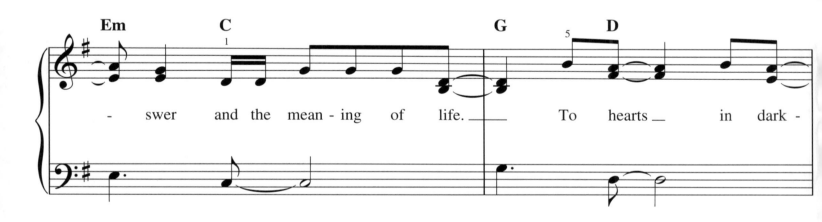

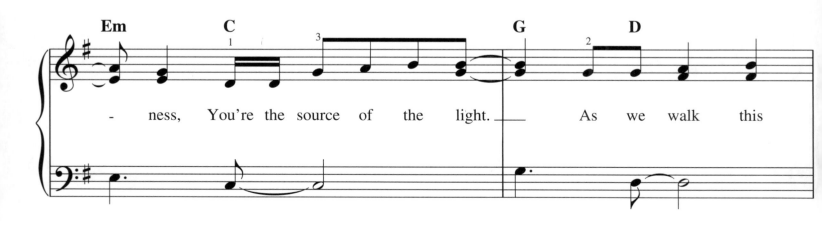

me (when I had no way.) _____ Res-cued my dy-ing heart _____ (that I could not save.) _____

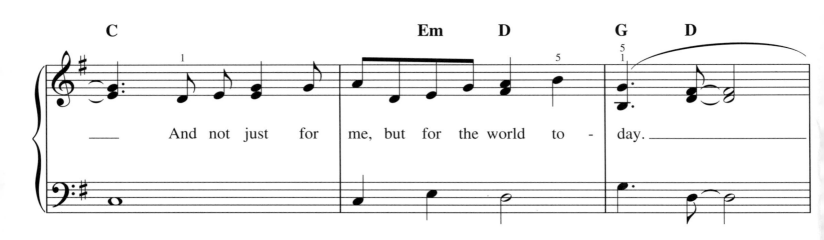

_____ And not just for me, but for the world to - day. _____

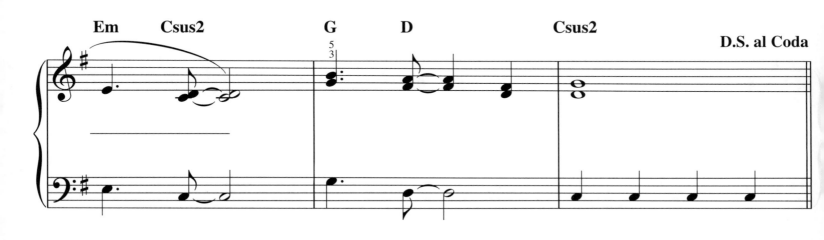

D.S. al Coda

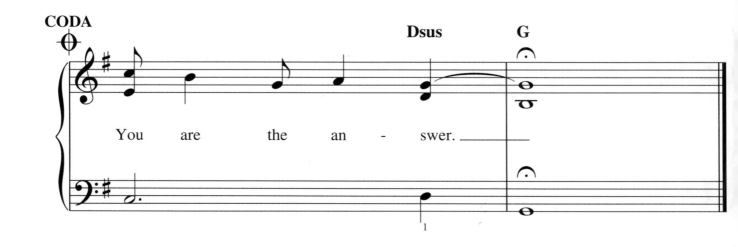

CODA

You are the an - swer. _____

TAKE YOU AT YOUR WORD

Words and Music by GRANT CUNNINGHAM
and PAUL FIELD

The more I
I've heard the

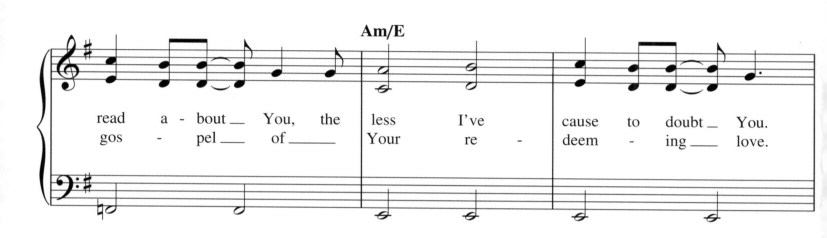

read a - bout __ You, the less I've cause to doubt __ You.
gos - pel __ of __ Your re - deem - ing __ love.

What You say, Lord, __ You mean. __ Now __
What You say, Lord, __ You do. I know __

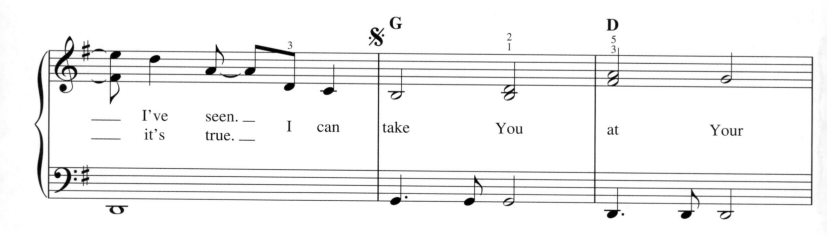

__ I've seen. __ I can take You at Your
__ it's true. __

Your word is love, Your word is true.

Your word is life, Your word is love, Your word

is true. Say, You say Your word.

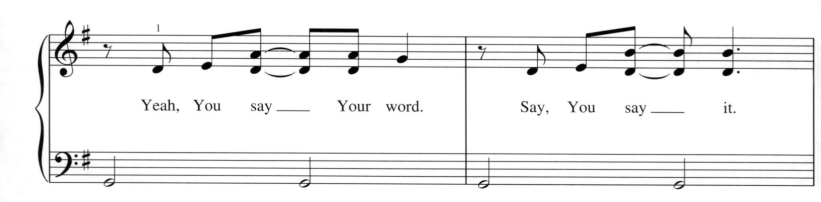

Yeah, You say Your word. Say, You say it.

Yeah, yeah, yeah._____ Say, You say_____ Your word.

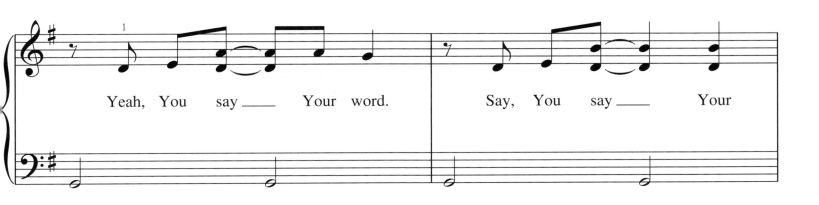

Yeah, You say_____ Your word. Say, You say_____ Your

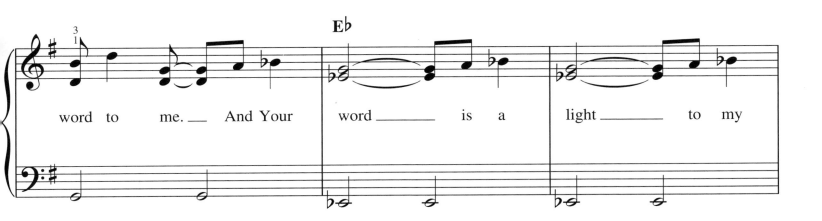

Eb

word to me.____ And Your word_____ is a light_____ to my

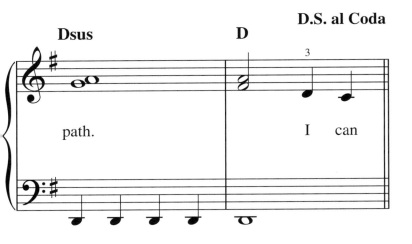

Dsus   D   D.S. al Coda

path.   I can

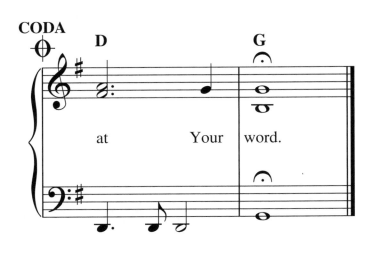

CODA   D   G

at   Your word.

The BEST Easy Worship Songbooks

THE BEST PRAISE & WORSHIP SONGS EVER

74 all-time favorites: Awesome God • Breathe • Days of Elijah • Here I Am to Worship • I Could Sing of Your Love Forever • Open the Eyes of My Heart • Shout to the Lord • We Bow Down • dozens more.

00311312 P/V/G..$19.95

THE BIG-NOTE WORSHIP BOOK

20 worship tunes for beginning players, including: Agnus Dei • Days of Elijah • Everlasting God • Friend of God • Give Us Clean Hands • Here I Am to Worship • Mighty to Save • Open the Eyes of My Heart • Sing to the King • and more.

00311875 Big-Note Piano.........................$10.99

CONTEMPORARY WORSHIP FAVORITES

The Phillip Keveren Series
Easy arrangements of 15 powerful Christian favorites: Beautiful One • Better Is One Day • Breathe • Friend of God • Grace Flows Down • I Give You My Heart • Indescribable • Once Again • Revelation Song • The Wonderful Cross • and more.

00311805 Easy Piano...............................$12.95

THE EASY WORSHIP FAKE BOOK

This beginning fake book includes over 100 songs, all in the key of "C" with simplified chords. Songs include: Above All • Come, Now Is the Time to Worship • He Is Exalted • Lord, I Lift Your Name on High • You're Worthy of My Praise • and dozens more.

00240265 Melody/Lyrics/Chords $19.95

HERE I AM TO WORSHIP – FOR KIDS

This addition to the WorshipTogether series lets the kids join in on the best modern worship songs. Includes 20 favorites: Awesome God • Breathe • God of Wonders • He Is Exalted • Wonderful Maker • You Are My King (Amazing Love) • and more.

00316098 Easy Piano...............................$14.95

HOW GREAT IS OUR GOD

The Phillip Keveren Series
Keveren's big-note arrangements of 15 praise & worship favorites: Above All • Awesome God • Days of Elijah • Forever • Give Thanks • Here I Am to Worship • The Potter's Hand • Shout to the Lord • We Fall Down • more.

00311402 Big-Note Piano.........................$12.95

MODERN HYMNS

Easy piano arrangements of 20 contemporary worship favorites: Amazing Grace (My Chains Are Gone) • Before the Throne of God Above • How Deep the Father's Love for Us • In Christ Alone • Take My Life • The Wonderful Cross • and more.

00311859 Easy Piano...............................$12.99

MORE OF THE BEST PRAISE & WORSHIP SONGS EVER

Simplified arrangements of 80 more contemporary worship favorites, including: Beautiful One • Everlasting God • Friend of God • Hear Our Praises • In Christ Alone • The Power of Your Love • Your Grace Is Enough • Your Name • and more.

00311801 Easy Piano...............................$19.99

MY FIRST WORSHIP BOOK

Beginning pianists will love the five-finger piano format used in this songbook featuring eight worship favorites: Friend of God • Give Thanks • Here I Am to Worship • I Will Call Upon the Lord • More Precious Than Silver • Sing to the King • We Fall Down • and more.

00311874 Five-Finger Piano $7.99

PRAISE & WORSHIP FAVORITES

8 arrangements that even beginners can enjoy, including: Ancient of Days • Breathe • Change My Heart Oh God • Come, Now Is the Time to Worship • Here I Am to Worship • Open the Eyes of My Heart • Shine, Jesus, Shine • There Is None like You.

00311271 Beginning Piano Solo $9.95

TIMELESS PRAISE

The Phillip Keveren Series
20 songs of worship wonderfully arranged for easy piano by Phillip Keveren: As the Deer • El Shaddai • Give Thanks • How Beautiful • How Majestic Is Your Name • Lord, I Lift Your Name on High • Shine, Jesus, Shine • There Is a Redeemer • Thy Word • and more.

00310712 Easy Piano...............................$12.95

TODAY'S WORSHIP HITS

16 modern worship favorites, including: Amazed • Beautiful One • Days of Elijah • How Great Is Our God • Sing to the King • and more.

00311439 Easy Piano...............................$10.95

WORSHIP FAVORITES

20 powerful songs arranged for big-note piano: Above All • Forever • Here I Am to Worship • Open the Eyes of My Heart • Shout to the Lord • and dozens more.

00311207 Big-Note Piano.........................$10.95

WORSHIP TOGETHER FAVORITES FOR KIDS

This folio features 12 easy arrangements of today's most popular worship songs: Enough • Everlasting God • Forever • How Great Is Our God • Made to Worship • Mountain of God • Wholly Yours • The Wonderful Cross • Yes You Have • You Never Let Go • and more.

00316109 Easy Piano...............................$12.95